INSTANT
GERMAN

by Dorothy and David Thomas

Editorial Consultant
Marianne Yasuda-Buser

Illustrated by DRAGONFLY DESIGNS

dot publications

About the Authors

David Thomas studied at Oxford University and London. Dorothy Thomas was a student at the Universities of Newcastle upon Tyne, Oslo and Bonn, and is a member of the Institute of Linguists.

While teaching Norwegian to adult students in London, Dorothy found that many had never learned another language. She developed the method used in this book so that they were able to talk with confidence right from the beginning. Grammar came later, after students had learned the basics of the language and could see how it all fitted together.

When not travelling the world talking to people, Dorothy's main interest is music, while David is an *aficionado* of rail travel.

New edition 1992
Copyright ©DM & DWS Thomas 1990,1992

Published by dot Publications
54A Haig Avenue, Whitley Bay NE25 8JD, Great Britain

ISBN 1 871086 06 x

Printed in the U.K. by Charter Press Ltd., Rhuddlan, North Wales

Deutschland - Germany

der Schweiz - Switzerland

Österreich - Austria

Bayreuth	- By-**royt**	Mainz	- Mine-ts
Braunschweig	- **Brown**sh-vighe	München	- **Muwn**shen
Köln	- Kurln	Wien	- Veen
Leipzig	- **Lipe**-tsish	Zürich	- **Tsuw**rish

3

Contents

Introduction

If you've never spoken a word of a foreign language before, or you've forgotten everything you learned at school, your problems are now (mostly) over.

Inside the back cover you'll find a list of basic phrases which you can use in all sorts of circumstances.

First look up what you need in the **Contents** section or the **Index**, then just follow the speech guides beneath each picture.

Use the guide on page 6 to help you say it correctly. As well as the pronunciation, we show you where to put the emphasis by setting the right part of a word in **heavy** type.

Next we take you through a series of typical tourist situations, giving you the words you'll need to get what you want, followed by some idea of the replies you are likely to hear.

In most cases we give you a basic situation which can be used in lots of places - for example, the phrases used in the baker's shop on page 28 can be used to buy things in most other kinds of shop too.

If you want to go a little further with the language, at the back you will find a short section explaining the most important points of German grammar.

Right at the back, on page 80, is a list of numbers. Learn these first if you can - numbers are a vital part of any language and will mean that shopping, making arrangements and just talking to people are very much easier.

Remember, travel abroad should be fun, and making your way in the local language is a big part of it. We aim to help you enjoy yourself on your trip.

Gute Reise!

German Sounds

We have tried to keep our transcription simple, so that you can read all the questions and answers almost as if they were English. Some words are split by a hyphen to make them easier to read and to get the stress in the right place. Pronounce them as one word, with no gaps. *Stress*: letters printed in **heavy** type should be stressed. *Compound words:* German very often joins several words together, e.g. *Kartoffelsalat* - potato salad, so be prepared to look under more than one heading.

ai, ei sound like eye.
au rhymes with how.
äu, eu rhyme with boy.
a can be long or short, but is like **a** in father.
ä like **e** in met.
b as in English, but **p** at the end of a word or syllable.

c like **c** in cat, but like **ts** in lets before e, i, ä, ö.
ch after a, o, u it's the throaty sound of **ch** in loch. After e, i, l, n, r it's the same sound as **h** in huge. (For simplicity, we have represented this by the southern **sh**.)
d as in English, but **t** at the end of a word or syllable.
e short as in m**e**t, long as in date. At the end of a word it's like a in Emma.

g as in **g**o, but **-ig** at the end of a word is pronounded the same as **ich**. After **n** it's as in singer, never like finger.
i as in bit.
ie as in piece.
j like **y** in yes.
kn sounds almost as if there is a very short **uh** (like the u in nut) between the k and the n, like king Canute.
o short as in hot, when long it's as in note.
ö like **ur** in fur, but the r is barely pronounced.

pf works the same way as **kn**.
qu sounds like **k+v**.
s is like **z** at the beginning of a word or syllable, **sh** before p or t. At the end of a word or syllable, or before a consonant, **s** and **ss** sound like **s** in glass.
ß sounds like **ss**.
sch like **sh** in ship.
tsch like **ch** in chip.

u can be long or short and resembles **oo** in good.
ü like the French **u** in tu: purse your lips quite tightly as if you are going to whistle.
v is pronounced **f**
w is pronounced **v**.
y sounds the same as **ü**.
z like **ts** in lets.

Booking Accommodation

Sehr geehrte Herren! Dear Sirs,

Hotels: *Ich möchte ein/zwei Einzelzimmer/Doppelzimmer (mit Bad) für —*
Nächte vom — bis zum — reservieren.
I should like to book one/two single/double room(s) (with bath) for —
nights from — to —

Camping: *Ich möchte einen Platz (gerne mit Stromanschluß), auf Ihrem*
Campingplatz reservieren. Wir möchten — Nächte vom — bis zum —
bleiben.
I should like to book a pitch (with electricity) on your campsite. We wish to
stay — nights from — to —.

Wir haben ein Auto/einen Wohnwagen/ein Wohnmobil und ein großes/
kleines Zelt.
We have a car/caravan/motor caravan and a large/small tent.

Bitte, wieviel müssen wir hinterlegen, um den Platz zu reservieren?
How much deposit do we need to book the pitch?

Unsere Gruppe/Familie wird aus — Erwachsene und — Kinder bestehen.
Our group/family will consist of — adults and — children.

Bitte auch Ihre Preise anzugeben.
Please let us know your prices.

Hochachtungsvoll,
Yours sincerely,

HOTELS

Germany has a wide variety of accommodation. A **Schloßhotel** is a converted castle or palace, **Rasthof** or **Raststätte** means motel, a **Gasthof** or **Gasthaus** is an inn and a **Pension** or **Fremdenheim** is a boarding house. All these serve meals.

NOTE: A **Hotel garni** only serves breakfast; a **Gaststätte** is a restaurant only; **credit cards:** few pensions and not all hotels accept these (to check, see p.35).

RECEPTION: look for Rezeption – Empfang – Anmeldung.

If you've booked

1. Guten Abend.
2. Ich habe bei Ihnen ein Zimmer bestellt.
4. Mein Name ist Philip Jones.
3. Wie ist Ihr Name, bitte?
5. Moment, bitte. Ja, Zimmer Nummer zehn. Könnten Sie bitte unterschreiben?

REZEPTION

1. *Gooten aabent.*
   Good evening.
2. *Ish haaba by **ee**nen ine tsimma besh**telt.***
   I have booked a room here.
4. *Mine naama ist Philip Jones.*
   My name is Philip Jones.

3. *Vee ist eer naama, bitta?*
   What is your name, please?
5. *Mo**ment**, bitta. Yah, tsimma numma tsayn. **Kurn**ten zee bitta **oon**ta-**shry**ben?*
   Just a moment. Yes, room number 10. Please sign here.

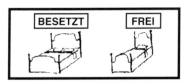

BESETZT   FREI

If you **haven't** booked, the key words are **frei** (vacant) and **besetzt** or **belegt** (full). The receptionist may say "Es tut mir leid" *(Ess toot meer lite)* I'm sorry, or "leider" *(**lie**-da)* sorry, or "kein" *(kine)* none.

If you want a **room,** look for any variation on **Zimmer** (room/s). In most towns the Tourist Information Office will make a booking for you (virtually all speak English).
Look for **Verkehrsamt** *(fur-**kayr**zamt),* **Verkehrsbüro / verein, Kurverwaltung, Auskunft,** or this sign –
The accommodation bureau is: **Zimmernachweis** or **Zimmervermittlung.**

eine Nacht · zwei Nächte
eye-na nakht · tsv-**eye** nekhta
one night · two nights

1. Guten Tag. Haben Sie ein Zimmer frei?
2. Ja, für wieviele Personen?
3. Zwei Personen und ein Kind (zwei Kinder).
4. Für wie lange, bitte?
5. Für eine Nacht (eine Woche).

1. **Goo**ten taag. **Haa**ben zee ine tsimma fry?
   Hello. Have you a room available?

3. Tsv-**eye** pair**zon**en oont ine kint (tsv-**eye** kinnda).
   Two people and one child (two children).

2. Yah, fewr veefeela pair**zon**en?
   Yes, how many for?

4. Fewr vee langa, bitta?
   How long for?

5. Fewr eye-na nakht (eye-na vokha).
   For one night (one week).

Einzelzimmer
ine-tsel tsimma
single

Doppelzimmer
doppel tsimma
double

das Bad
dass baat
the bath

die Dusche
dee doosha
the shower

die Toilette
dee twa-**lett**a
the lavatory

1. Ein Einzelzimmer oder ein Doppelzimmer?
2. Ein Doppelzimmer und zwei Einzelzimmer.
3. Mit oder ohne Bad?
4. Mit Bad, bitte.

1. Ine **ine**-tsel tsimma oda ine **dopp**el tsimma?
   A single room or a double?

3. Mit oda ohna baat?
   With or without bath?

2. Ine **dopp**el tsimma oont tsv-**eye** ine-tsel tsimma.
   A double and two singles.

4. Mit baat, bitta.
   With bath, please.

9

1. *Vass kostet dass tsimma?*
   How much is the room?

3. *Yah, dass nayma ish.*
   Fine, I'll take it.

2. *Pro pair**zone** – mark, mit **frew-shtewk**.*
   — marks per person, with breakfast.

4. *Vo kan ish here parken?*
   Where can I park?

mein Paß
mine pass
my passport

1. *Alzo, vee ist eer naama, bitta?*
   Right, what is your name please?

3. ***Kurn**ten zee bitta **oon**ta-**shry**ben?*
   Could you sign here, please?

4. *Zo, danka.*
   *Here ist eer **shluw**-sel.*
   Thank you.
   Here is your key.

2. *Mine naama ist Helen Baker.*
   My name is Helen Baker.

★

Meinen Schlüssel, bitte,
Zimmer Nummer achtzehn.

***My**nen **shluw**-sel, bitta,*
*tsimma numma **akht**-tsayn.*
Could I have my key, please?
Room number 18.

10

Inspecting the room

1. Darf ich das Zimmer sehen?
2. Ja, gern.
3. Gut, ich nehme es.

– OR –

4. (a) Nein, es gefällt mir nicht.
   (b) Es ist zu klein.
   (c) Ich möchte ein ruhiges Zimmer.

5. Können Sir mir noch ein anderes Zimmer anzeigen?

6. Es tut mir leid ...

1. *Darf ish dass tsimma* **zay**-*en?*
   May I see the room?
2. *Yah, gairn.*
   Yes, certainly.

3. *Goot, ish nayma ess.* – OR –
   Good, I'll take it.
4. (a) *Nine, ess ghe**felt** meer nisht.*
   (b) *Ess ist tsoo kline.*
   (c) *Ish murshta ine **roo**-igges tsimma.*
   (a) No, I don't like it.
   (b) It's too small
   (c) I want a quiet room.

5. ***Kur**nen zee meer nokh ine **anda**-res tsimma **ar:ts**-eye-ghen?*
   Could you show me another room?

6. *Ess toot meer lite ...*
   I'm sorry ...

Hotel meals

1. Wann kann ich frühstücken?
   (Mittagessen, Abendessen)
2. Von sechs Uhr bis neun Uhr dreißig.

Checking out

1. Kann ich bitte meine Rechnung haben?
2. Herzlichen Dank für alles!
3. Auf Wiedersehen!

1. *Van can ish **frew**-shtewken?*
   (***mitt**aag-**ess**en, **aa**bent-**ess**en)*
   What time do you serve breakfast? (lunch, supper)

2. *Fon zex oor biss noyn oor **dry**-sish.*
   From 6 o'clock to 9.30.

(Check the time on p.73)

1. *Can ish bitta my-na **rekh**noong haaben?*
   Please may I have the bill.

2. ***Hair**ts-likhen dank fewr **al**-less!*
   Thank you very much for everything!

3. *Owf **vee**da-zane!*
   Goodbye!

(Methods of payment p.35)

RENTED ACCOMMODATION

You will generally know the name of your landlord or landlady, so just ask:

1. Entschuldigen Sie bitte, wo wohnt Frau — ?

OR

2. Ich suche Herrn —

1. *Ent-**shool**diggen zee bitta,*
   vo vohnt Frow –?
   Excuse me,
   where does Mrs. — live?

2. *Ish zookha Hairn –*
   I'm looking for Mr. —

Once inside:

Die Küche – *Dee **Kuw**sha* – The Kitchen

die Schlüssel
*dee **shluw**-sel*
the keys

die Heizung
*dee **hy**-tsoong*
the heating

Warm/Kaltwasser
*varm/kalt **vass**er*
hot/cold water

der Garten
*dair **gar**ten*
the garden

die Tür
dee tuwr
the door

der Herd
dair hairt
the cooker

der Ausguß
*dair **owss**goose*
the sink

1. Der Herd geht nicht.

2. Bringen Sie mir bitte (eine Decke).

1. *Dair hairt gate nisht.*
   The cooker is not working/
   broken.

2. ***Bring**en zee meer bitta*
   (eye-na decka).
   Could you get me (a blanket),
   please.

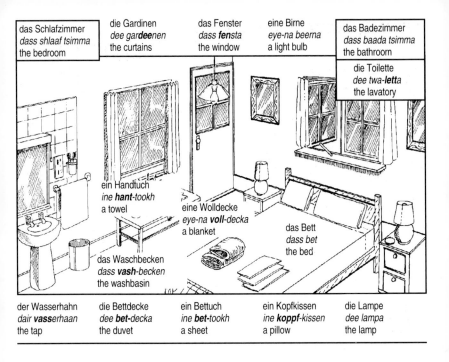

das Schlafzimmer	die Gardinen	das Fenster	eine Birne	das Badezimmer
dass shlaaf tsimma	*dee gardeenen*	*dass fensta*	*eye-na beerna*	*dass baada tsimma*
the bedroom	the curtains	the window	a light bulb	the bathroom

die Toilette
dee twa-letta
the lavatory

ein Handtuch
ine hant-tookh
a towel

eine Wolldecke
eye-na voll-decka
a blanket

das Bett
dass bet
the bed

das Waschbecken
dass vash-becken
the washbasin

der Wasserhahn	die Bettdecke	ein Bettuch	ein Kopfkissen	die Lampe
dair vasserhaan	*dee bet-decka*	*ine bet-tookh*	*ine koppf-kissen*	*dee lampa*
the tap	the duvet	a sheet	a pillow	the lamp

ein Glas
ine glass
a glass

ein Teller
ine teller
a plate

ein Topf
ine toppf
a pan

eineTasse
eye-na tassa
a cup

eine Bratpfanne
eye-na brat-pfanna
a frying pan

der Abfall	der Kühlschrank	ein Stuhl	eine Gabel	die Kaffee/Teekanne
dair appfal	*dair kuwl-shrank*	*ine shtool*	*eye-na gaabel*	*dee kaffay/tày kanna*
the rubbish	the refrigerator	a chair	a fork	the coffee/teapot
ein Geschirrtuch	der Tisch	die Kanne	ein Messer	ein Löffel
ine gesheer-tookh	*dair tish*	*dee kanna*	*ine messer*	*ine lurfel*
a tea-towel	the table	the jug	a knife	a spoon

CAMPING

CAMPING 200m▶

Entschuldigen Sie bitte, wo ist der Campingplatz?

CAMPING EUROPA

2. Ja, für wie lange, bitte?

BÜRO ⌐ REZEPTION

1. Haben Sie noch Platz?
(für ein Zelt/einen Wohnwagen/ ein Wohnmobil).

3. Eine Nacht (zwei Nächte/eine Woche).

---

*Ent-**shool**diggen zee bitta, vo ist dair camping plats?*
Excuse me, where is the campsite?

1. ***Haa**ben zee nokh plats? (fewr ine tselt/**eye**-nen **vone** vaaghen/ine **vone**-mobeel.*
Have you any room? (for a tent/caravan/ motor caravan).

2. *Yah, fewr vee langa, bitta?*
Yes, how long would you like to stay?

3. *Eye-na nakht (tsv-**eye** nekhta/eye-na vokha).*
One night (two nights/a week).

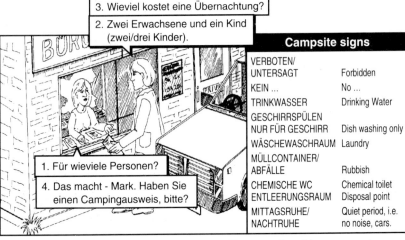

3. Wieviel kostet eine Übernachtung?

2. Zwei Erwachsene und ein Kind (zwei/drei Kinder).

1. Für wieviele Personen?

4. Das macht - Mark. Haben Sie einen Campingausweis, bitte?

Campsite signs

VERBOTEN/ UNTERSAGT	Forbidden
KEIN ...	No ...
TRINKWASSER	Drinking Water
GESCHIRRSPÜLEN NUR FÜR GESCHIRR	Dish washing only
WÄSCHEWASCHRAUM	Laundry
MÜLLCONTAINER/ ABFÄLLE	Rubbish
CHEMISCHE WC ENTLEERUNGSRAUM	Chemical toilet Disposal point
MITTAGSRUHE/ NACHTRUHE	Quiet period, i.e. no noise, cars.

---

1. *Fewr vee**fee**la pair**zon**en?*
How many are there of you?

4. *Dass makht — mark. **Haa**ben zee **eye**-nen camping **owss**-vice, bitta?*
That will be - marks.
Have you a carnet, please?

2. *Tsv-**eye** air-**vakh**senna oont ine kint (tsv-**eye**/dry kinnda).*
Two adults and one child (two/three children).

3. *Veefeel **kost**et eye-na **uw**ber-**nakh**toong?*
How much does it cost per night?

1. *Ish **brow**-kha **eye**-nen*
   ***shtrome**-anshlooss datt**soo**.*
   I'd like electricity (a hook-up)
   too.

2. *Oom veefeel oor **makh**en zee*
   ***aa**bends **tsoo**?*
   What time do you close in the
   evenings?

3. *Oom halp elf.*
   At 10.30 (Time: p.73).

International Camping Carnet

Widely accepted at campsites overseas as
an identity document. Though seldom
obligatory, it is useful not to have to leave
your passport in reception. You'll need it for
things like changing money, after all.

Youth Hostel/Mountain Hut

die Jugendherberge	die Berghütte
*dee **Yoo**ghent-hair**bair**ga*	*dee **Bairg**-huwta*
the Youth Hostel	the Mountain Hut

Herbergsvater (mutter)
***Hair**bairgs-faata (mootta)*
male (female) warden

1. ***Goo**ten **aa**bent. **Haa**ben zee nokh*
   fry-a pletza?
   Good evening. Have you any
   room?

2. *Ish murshta eye-na nakht (tsv-**eye***
   *nekhta) **bly**-ben.*
   I'd like to stay one night (two).

3. *Here ist mine **mit**gleeds-**owss**vice.*
   Here is my membership card.

4. ***Haa**ben zee **bett**vesha?*
   *(**eye**-nen **shlaaf**sack).*
   Have you any bedlinen?
   (a sleeping bag).

EATING OUT

Eating is one of the pleasures of going to Germany and there's no shortage of food or places to enjoy it.

COFFEE, CAKES, ICE CREAM, SNACKS (p.18): Any **Café** or **Konditorei** serves these. Choose your cake at the counter, take your ticket (**Bon**), then sit down and order drinks and it will be brought to you. You can often get breakfast here too, together with the daily newspapers. The Austrian version is **Kaffeehaus** and in Switzerland it's a **Tea-room**.

Large towns have inexpensive standing COFFEE-only bars too.

TAKE-AWAYS AND FAST FOOD (p.26): **Schnellimbiss** *(shnell-imbiss)*, **Straßenverkauf** and **zum Mitnehmen**.

DRINKS (p.17): A **Bierstube** or **Weinstube** *(beer/vine shtooba)* often serves snacks as well. **Ein großes/kleines Bier** *(ine grocers/klynas beer)* means a large/small glass of beer (in Austria a Weinstube is a **Heuriger—hoy**rigga).

MEALS: **(durchgehend) warme Küche:** hot food/snacks (all day).
          gut bürgerliche Küche: good home cooking.

Anywhere whose name includes **Speise** serves meals. Most department stores have a cafeteria too.

Different kinds of RESTAURANTS (pp.19-25) are: **Gaststätte** *(gast—shtetta)*, **Gasthaus/hof, Raststätte/hof** and **Ratskeller** (this is in the town hall; Rathaus: Rat – *raat* = advice, it's not a comment on the cooking!).

MEALTIMES:
Frühstück *(frew-shtewk)* — breakfast
Mittagessen *(mittaag-essen)* — main meal, served about 12.00-2.00 p.m.
Abendessen *(aabent-essen)* — served 6.30-8.30/9.00 p.m.

CLOSED? Geschlossen? Most places have a rest day (Ruhetag or Betriebsruhe) once a week.

TWO = Zwei/zwo. When ordering, zwo is often used instead of zwei to avoid confusion with drei (three).

Guten Appetit!   Prost!/Zum Wohl!
*Goo*ten appa-**teet!**   *Prohst!/Tsoom* **vole!**
Enjoy your meal!   Cheers!

★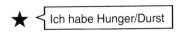

Ish haaba hoong-a/doorst.
I'm hungry/thirsty.

Basic ordering 1: Drinks

Apfelsaft
Apfel-zaft
apple juice

Johannisbeersaft
Yohanniss-bayrzaft
blackcurrant juice

Limonade
Limmonaada
lemonade

Orangensaft
Oranshenzaft
orange juice

Traubensaft
Trowben-zaft
grape juice

Zitronensaft
Tsit-roh-nenzaft
lemon juice

Bier (vom Faß)
Beer (fom fass)
(draught) beer

Rot (weiß) wein
Rote (vice) vine
red (white) wine

More drinks p.24.

> 1. Herr Ober! (Fräulein!)
> 2. Guten Tag, bitte schön?
> 3. Ein Bier, bitte.
> 4. Ein Großes oder ein Kleines?
> 5. Ein kleines Bier, einen Apfelsaft, eine Cola und ein Glas Weißwein, bitte.

1. *Hair oba! (Froyline!)*
   Waiter! (Waitress!)
2. *Gooten taag, bitta shurn?*
   Hallo, what would you like?
3. *Ine beer, bitta.*
   A beer, please.
4. *Ine grocers oda ine klynas?*
   A large one or a small one?
5. *Ine klynas beer, eye-nen apfel-zaft, eye-na Cola oont ine glass vicevine, bitta.*
   A small beer, an apple juice, a Coke and a glass of white wine, please.

Paying, finding the lavatory

> 2. Wo ist die Toilette?
> 1. Danke schön! Wieviel?

★

| Ist hier noch frei? |

Ist here nokh fry?
Is this seat/table free?

1. *Danka shurn. Veefeel?*
   Thank you. How much is that?
2. *Vo ist dee twa-letta?*
   Where are the toilets?

17

Basic Ordering 2: Coffee and cakes, ice cream*

> 1. Guten Tag, bitte schön?
> 2. Ein Stück, bitte. Dies bitte!
> 3. Mit (Schlag) Sahne?
> 4. Noch etwas?

1. **Goo**ten taag, bitta shurn?
   Hallo, what would you like?

2. Ine shtuwk, bitta. Deess, bitta!
   One (piece) please.
   That one, please.

3. Mit (Schlaag) zaana?
   With (whipped) cream?

4. Nokh **et**vass?
   Anything else?

*see also p.25

Kuchen/Torten – Cakes

Schwarzwälder Kirschtorte
sh**varts**velda **keersh** torta
Black Forest cherry cake

Berliner
bair**lee**na
doughnut

Obsttorte
oabst torta
fruit tart

Käsesahne
kayza zaana
cheese cake

Pflaumenschnitte
pf**low**-men shnitta
plum slice

> 1. (Ich möchte) Kaffee, bitte.
> 3. Ein Kännchen, bitte, ein Glas Tee und zwei Eis.
> 4. Danke schön. Die Rechnung, bitte.
> 2. Tasse oder Kännchen?

1. (Ish murshta) kaff**ay**, bitta.
   (I'd like) coffee, please.

2. Tassa oda **kenn**shen?
   A cup or a pot?

3. Ine kennshen, bitta, ine glass tay
   oont tsv-**eye** ice.
   A pot, a glass of tea and two ice
   creams, please.

4. Danka shurn. Dee **rekh**noong, bitta.
   Thank you. May I have the bill,
   please.

zweimal Kaffee
tsv-**eye**-mal kaffay
two coffees

mit Zucker (Eis)
mit tsookka (ice)
with sugar (ice)

Tee (mit Zitrone)
tay (mit tsit-**rona**)
tea (with lemon)

Breakfast

1. *Gooten morgen. Vass murshten zee, bitta?*
   Good morning. What would you like?

2. *Ish murshta (veer murshten) frew-shtewken, bitta.*
   I (we) would like breakfast, please.

3. *Kaffay oda tay?*
   Tea or coffee?

4. *Nokh etvass — bitta.*
   Some more — please.

heiße/kalte Milch *hy-sa/kalta milsh* hot/cold milk	Käse *kayza* cheese	Brot/Brötchen/Toast *brote/brurtshen/toast* bread/rolls/toast	ein (weiches) Ei *ine (vyshess) eye* a (soft-boiled) egg
	Wurst (Aufschnitt) *voorst (owf-shnitt)* sausage (cold meat)		Spiegelei *shpeegel eye* fried egg
			Rührei *rua eye* scrambled egg

Restaurants — Booking a table

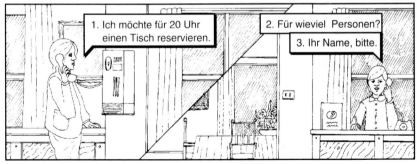

1. *Ish murshta fewr ts-vantsish oor eye-nen tish rezzairveeren.*
   I'd like to book a table for 8 o'clock.

2. *Fewr veefeel pairzonen?*
   How many for?

3. *Eer naama, bitta.*
   Your name, please.

Coping with 'phones p.41

19

... or just turning up on spec

1. Guten Tag (Abend). Haben Sie einen Tisch für drei?

2. Moment, bitte ... Haben Sie reserviert?

1. **Goo**ten taag (**aa**bent). **Haab**en zee **eye**-nen tish fewr dry?
   Hallo (good evening). Have you a table for three?

2. Mo-**ment**, bitta ...
   Haaben zee rezzair**veert**?
   Just a moment ... Have you booked?

Ordering a meal

1. Guten Tag. Was ist das Tagesgericht, bitte?

2. Zweimal Gulaschsuppe, bitte.

3. Ich möchte bitte ein Sahnesteak mit Pommes frites und Salat.

4. Und für das Kind (die Kinder), was können Sie da empfehlen?

5. Möchten Sie noch einen Nachtisch?

1. **Goo**ten taag. Vass ist dass **taa**gas-ghe**risht**, bitta?
   Hallo. What is today's special, please?

3. Ish murshta bitta ine zaana steak mit pom fritt oont za**laat**.
   I'd like steak in cream sauce with chips/fries and salad.

2. Tsv-**eye**-mal **goo**lash zuppa, bitta.
   Two goulash soups, please.

4. Oont fewr dass kint (dee **kinn**da), vass **kur**nen zee da emp**fay**len?
   And what do you recommend for the child (the children)?

5. **Mursh**ten zee nokh **eye**-nen **nakh**-tish?
   Would you like dessert?

(See pp.21-23 for a selection of things you might order, and p.24 for drinks).

In the Restaurant: This is the sort of thing you'll meet.

Speisekarte — 1

dee Shpyser-karta — die Speisekarte — **MENU**

Long words: Since German often runs words together, you may need to look under more than one section to find out what you are eating.

Side dishes p.23. Sausages and Snacks p.26.

Tagesspezialitäten — Dishes of the Day

SUPPEN — Soup   *VORSPEISEN — Starters*

Erbsensuppe
airpsen zuppa
Split pea soup

Leberknödelsuppe
layba knurdle zuppa
Liver and dumpling soup

Gulaschsuppe
goolash zuppa
Goulash soup

Tagessuppe
taagas zuppa
Soup of the day

Hühnerbrühe
huwna bruw-a
Chicken broth

Zwiebelsuppe
tsveeble zuppa
Onion soup

Russische Eier
roossisha eye-a
Russian eggs

Aufschnittplatte
owfshnit platta
Cold meat selection

SCHNITZEL — Veal escalope

There are dozens of different varieties of Schnitzel in German-speaking parts of Europe. Here are just a few of the commoner varieties to be getting on with.

Jägerschnitzel
yayga shnitzel
with mushrooms

(Schweineschnitzel)
(shvyna shnitzel)
(Pork fillet)

Wienerschnitzel
veena shnitzel
in breadcrumbs

Rahmschnitzel
raam shnitzel
in cream sauce

Zigeunerschnitzel
tsiggoyna shnitzel
with peppers

Haben Sie
vegetarische Kost?

★

Haaben zee
vayghe-**taa**risha cost?
Have you any vegetarian dishes?

HAUPTGERICHTE —
Main Dishes

vom Kalb — Veal
vom Rind — Beef
vom Schwein — Pork

¹/₂ Brathähnchen
halbas braat hane-shen
¹/₂ roast chicken

(Gemüse) eintopf
(ghemuwza) inetoppf
(Vegetable) stew

Eisbein
ice bine
Pig's knuckle

Forelle blau
forrella bl-ow
Boiled trout

Frikadellen
frikkadellen
Meat patties

Geflügel Ragout
ghe-fluwgle raggoo
Chicken stew

Gefüllte Paprikaschote
ghe-fuwlta paprika shoata
Stuffed pepper

Gemischtes vom Grill
ghemishtas fom grill
Mixed grill

Hacksteak — hacksteak
(see Schnitzels)
Chopped steak

Hasenkeule
haazen koyla
Leg of hare

Klopse
kloppsa
Meatballs

Kotelett
kotta let
Chop

Eierspeisen — Egg Dishes (p.19)
Fisch — Fish
Fleisch — Meat
Käseteller — Cheese board
Kinderteller — for children

Leberkäs
layba kace
Pork and beef loaf

Lenden (spieß) braten
lenden (shpeece) braaten
Sirloin (spit) roasted

Matjesfilet
maatyes fillay
Herring fillet

Pfeffersteak
pfeffa steak
Peppered steak

Rinderbraten
rinnda braaten
Beef pot roast

Rindsrouladen
rints roolaaden
Beef olives

Rippchen
rippshen
Spare ribs

Sauerbraten
zower braaten
Pickled beef

Schweinebraten
shvyna braaten
Roast pork

Sülze
zuwl-tsa
Brawn

Tafelspitz
taafel shpitz
Boiled beef

You'll find a further selection
of Meat and Fish p.29.
Vegetables p.30-31.

BEILAGEN — Side dishes
NACH WAHL — to your choice

Bratkartoffeln
braat kartoffeln
Fried potatoes

Pommes frites
pom fritt
Chips/Fries

Champignons
shampeenyongs
Mushrooms

Reis
rice
Rice

Gemischter Salat
ghe-mishta zalaat
Mixed salad

Salzkartoffeln
zalts kartoffeln
Boiled potatoes

Gurkensalat
goorken zalaat
Cucumber salad

Sauerkraut
zower krowt
Pickled cabbage

Klösse/Knödel
klursa/knurdle
Dumplings

Spargel
shpargle
Asparagus

Nudeln
noodeln
Noodles

Spätzle
shpetsla
type of Pasta

Pilze
piltsa
Mushrooms

Speckbohnen
shpeck boanen
Beans with ham

NACHSPEISEN — Desserts
Frische Ananas/Erdbeeren
frisha anna-nass/airtbayren
Fresh pineapple/strawberries

Fruchtbecher
frukht besher
Fruit sundae

Gemischtes Eis
ghemishtas ice
Mixed ices

Kompott
kom-pot
Stewed fruit

Obstsalat
oabst zalaat
Fruit salad

Pfannkuchen
pfan-kooshen
Pancakes

Käseteller   *kayza-teller*   Cheese board

Ordering drinks *(Getränke)*

1. **Mursh**ten zee **et**vass tsoo **trink**en?
   Would you like anything to drink?

2. Bitta eye-na flasha **vice**vine *(**rote**vine).*
   A bottle of white (red) wine, please.

3. **Rhine**-vine oda **Moz**el-vine?
   Rhine or Moselle?

4. Mine**raal** vassa, bitta.
   Some mineral water, please.

5. Mit oda ohna **coa**len-zoyra?
   Fizzy or still?

Compliments, Complaints, Requests — and Paying

1. Bitta, nokh **et**vass brote.
   Some more bread, please.

2. Here faylt nokh ine besh**teck**.
   I/We need some more cutlery.

3. Hat ess ghesh**meckt**?
   Did you enjoy it?

4. Danka. **Owss**gets-**eye**-shnet!
   Yes, thank you, it was excellent.

5. Dee **resh**noong, bitta.
   May I have the bill, please.

6. Dass shine-t nisht tsoo sh**timm**en.
   I think there is a mistake.

Ice Cream

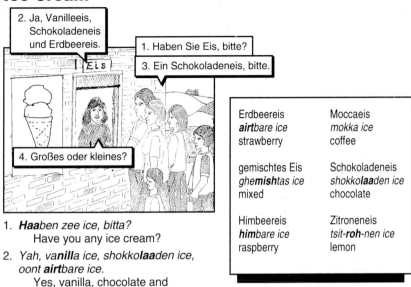

2. Ja, Vanilleeis, Schokoladeneis und Erdbeereis.

1. Haben Sie Eis, bitte?

3. Ein Schokoladeneis, bitte.

4. Großes oder kleines?

Erdbeereis *airtbare ice* strawberry	Moccaeis *mokka ice* coffee
gemischtes Eis *ghemishtas ice* mixed	Schokoladeneis *shokkolaaden ice* chocolate
Himbeereis *himbare ice* raspberry	Zitroneneis *tsit-roh-nen ice* lemon

1. *Haaben zee ice, bitta?*
   Have you any ice cream?

2. *Yah, vanilla ice, shokkolaaden ice, oont airtbare ice.*
   Yes, vanilla, chocolate and strawberry.

3. *Ine shokkolaaden ice, bitta.*
   A chocolate one, please.

4. *Grocers oda klynas?*
   Large or small?

Self-service/Choosing

1. Wie heißt dieses Gericht?

3. Und welche Gemüse?

2. (Ich möchte) etwas von dem, bitte.

4. Diese und jene.

1. *Vee hyste deezess gherisht?*
   What is this dish called?

2. *(Ish murshta) etvass fon dame, bitta.*
   (I'd like) some of that, please.

3. *Oont velsha ghemuwza?*
   And which vegetables?

4. *Deeza oont yayna.*
   These and those.

Fast Food *Warme/Kalte Speisen* Hot/Cold Snacks

A **Schnellimbiss** *(shnell-imbiss)* serves sausages (**Wurst**), chips (**Pommes frites** — *pom fritt* or *pommers*), mit Mayo (*my-o* — with mayonnaise), sandwiches (**belegte Brote** — *belaygta broata*), and hot and cold drinks. **Straßenverkauf** and **zum Mitnehmen** are also take-aways.

SCHNELLIMBISS

Würste: Sausages

KÄSEBROT
kayza brote
Open cheese sandwich

SCHINKEN
shinken
Ham

BLUTWURST
bloot voorst
Black pudding

BOCKWURST
bock voorst
long Frankfurter

POMMES FRITES
pom fritt
Chips/Fries

SENF
zenf
Mustard

WEIßWURST
vice voorst
Veal and bacon

BRATWURST	CURRYWURST	LEBERWURST	TEEWURST	ZERVELATW.
brat voorst	*curry voorst*	*layba voorst*	*tay voorst*	*tsairva-laatv.*
Fried, pork	Curry flavour	Liver sausage	Sausage spread	Salami-type

After you've eaten and digested, you may feel like ...

SHOPPING

geöffnet — open
Montag Ruhetag
Monday: rest day

geschlossen — closed
Mittwoch nachmittag geschlossen
closed Wednesday afternoon

OPENING TIMES: Shops open 8.30-9.00 a.m. and close at 6.00 or 6.30 p.m. On **Saturdays** shops close about 1.00 p.m. except the first Saturday of the month when they stay open all afternoon.

Look for the *Fußgängerzone* (pedestrian precinct) or the *Einkaufszentrum* (shopping centre), where you will find *der Markt (platz)* — the market (place). *Lebensmittel* means groceries, and any shop ending in *Markt* also sells food.

Selbstbedienung or *SB-Laden* is a self-service shop.

Reformhaus is not the prison, it sells health foods.

NOTE:

Use the pattern of conversation shown in the bakery for all other kinds of shopping.

Remember to say: Guten Tag — in South Germany and Austria Grüss Gott — when entering a shop, and Auf Wiedersehen when leaving.

SHOPPING: How to ask

Haben Sie (Äpfel?)
Haaben zee (epfell)?
Have you any (apples)?

Ich möchte bitte (Äpfel).
Ish murshta bitta (epfell).
I'd like some (apples) please.

ein Kilo Äpfel.
ine keelo epfell.
a kilo of apples.

hundert Gramm Butter.
hoondert gram bootta.
100 grammes (about 4ozs.) of butter.

ein halbes Kilo (ein Pfund) Tomaten.
ine halbas keelo (ine pfoont) tomaaten.
half a kilo of tomatoes (about 1lb.).

ein halbes Pfund käse
ine halbas pfoont kayza
about 8ozs. of cheese.

eine Scheibe (zwei Scheiben) Schinken.
eye-na shyba (tsv-eye shyben) shinken.
a slice (two slices) of ham.

Im Stück… oder geschnitten?
im shtewk oda gheshnitten?
Whole or in slices?

Ein Stück, bitte.
Ine shtuwk, bitta.
One, please.

Dies bitte!
Deece bitta!
That one please.

Die da.
Dee da.
Those.

Noch etwas.
Nokh etvass.
A little more.

Genug.
Ghenoog.
That's enough.

Das wär's.
Dass vayress.
That's all.

Sonst noch etwas?
Zonst nokh etvass?
Would you like anything else?

Was kostet das?
Vass kostet dass?
How much is it?

WEIGHTS & MEASURES

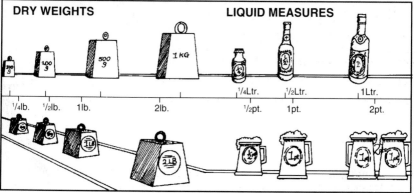

DRY WEIGHTS   **LIQUID MEASURES**

1 lb. = 454g.   **1 kg. = 2 lb. 3 ozs. approx.**   **1 Ltr. = 1³/₄ pts. approx.**

Bäckerei — *Becka-rye* — Baker

1. **Goo***ten* **mor***gen.*
   Good morning.

2. **Goo***ten* **mor***gen, bitta shurn?*
   Good morning, what would you like?

3. *Ish murshta gairna ine brote, bitta.*
   I'd like a loaf of bread, please.

4. *Ine* **kly***nas/grocers/***vice***-brote/*
   shvarts*-brote/***gr-ow***brote/*
   foll*kornbrote?*
   A small one/large one/white one black bread/rye/wholemeal?

5. *Deece bitta.*
   That one, please.

1. *Ish hetta gairna* **brurt***shen. Tsv-***eye** *shtewk, bitta.*
   I'd like some rolls.
   Two, please.

2. *Tsvo* **brurt***shen. Zonst nokh* **et***vass?*
   Two rolls. Anything else?

3. *Dass* **vay***ress. Vass makht dass?*
   That's all. How much is that?

4. *Dass makht — mark tsoo-***zammen.**
   That's — marks altogether.

5. *Bitta.*
   Here you are.

6. *Danka zayr. Owf* **vee***da zane!*
   Thanks very much. Goodbye.

*See note p.16

28

Metzgerei — *Metzga-rye* — Butcher
Fleisch
Meat

(in *German* order)

BEINSCHEIBE
bine shyba
Leg

FILET
fillay
Fillet

GANS
gance
Goose

GULASCH
goolash
seasoned Stewing
Steak

HACKFLEISCH
hack flysh
Mince

HÄHNCHEN/HUHN
hane-shen/hoon
Chicken

KOTELETT
kotta let
Chop

LEBER
layba
Liver

RINDFLEISCH
rint flysh
Beef

RIPPCHEN
ripshen
Ribs

SCHWEINEFLEISCH
shvyna flysh
Pork

SPECK
shpeck
Bacon

HAMMELFLEISCH
hammle flysh
Lamb

HASE
haaza
Hare

KALBFLEISCH
kalp flysh
Veal

WILD
villt
Game

Fische — Meeresfrüchte
Fisha — Mayress fruwhkta
Fish — Seafood

AAL
aal
Eel

DORSCH/
KABELJAU
dorsch/kaable-yow
Cod

FORELLE
forrella
Trout

HAIFISCH
high fish
Shark

HECHT
hekht
Pike

LACHS
lakhs
Salmon

MAKRELE
*ma**krayla***
Mackerel

ROTBARSCH
rote barsh
Red perch

SARDINEN
*zar**dee**nen*
Sardines

SCHOLLEN
schollen
Plaice

HERING
hayring
Herring

HUMMER
humma
Lobster

KARPFEN
Karpfen
Carp

KREBS
kreps
Crab

SPROTTEN
*sh**protten***
Sprats

29

Vegetables — Gemüse *(Ghemuwza)*

in *English* order

ARTISCHOKEN
*arti**shokk**en*
some Artichokes

SPARGEL
*sh**pargle***
some Asparagus

eine AVOCADO
***eye**-na **av**vokaado*
an Avocado

(grüne) BOHNEN
(gruwna) ***boa**nen*
(green) Beans

rote RÜBEN
*rota **ruw**ben*
some Beetroot

KOHL
coal
some Cabbage

MOHRRÜBEN
***moa**ruwben*
some Carrots

BLUMENKOHL
***bloo**men coal*
some Cauliflower

SELLERIE
***zell**eree*
some Celery

MAIS
mice
some corn

ÄPFEL
***ep**fell*
some Apples

APRIKOSEN
*appri**kozen***
some Apricots

BANANEN
*ba**naa**nen*
some Bananas

HEIDELBEEREN
***hy**del **bay**ren*
Blue-/bilberries

Fruit & Vegetables

(Ish murshta) — bitta
(Ich möchte) — bitte
(I'd like) — please

eine GURKE
*eye-na **goor**ka*
a cucumber

KNOBLAUCH
*k**nop** lowkh*
some Garlic

KOPFSALAT
*koppf za**laat***
a Lettuce

PILZE
piltza
some Mushrooms

ZWIEBELN
*ts**vee**beln*
some Onions

PETERSILIE
*payta-**zeel**ya*
some Parsley

Fruit — Obst *(Oabst)*

KIRSCHEN
keershen
some Cherries

STACHELBEEREN
shtakhel bayren
some Gooseberries

WEINTRAUBEN
vinetrow-ben
some Grapes

rote/schwarze
JOHANNISBEEREN
rota/shvartza
yohanniss bayren
Red/Blackcurrants

eine PAMPELMUSE
eye-na pample
mooza
a Grapefruit

eine ZITRONE
eye-na tsitrona
a Lemon

eine MELONE
eye-na maylona
a Melon

Obst und Gemüse

APFELSINEN
appfelzeenen
some Oranges

PFIRSICHE
pfeerzisha
some Peaches

BIRNEN
beernen
some Pears

eine ANANAS
eye-na annanass
a Pineapple

PFLAUMEN
pflowmen
some Plums

HIMBEEREN
himbayren
some
Raspberries

ERDBEEREN
airtbayren
some
Strawberries

RBSEN
irpzen
ome Peas

KARTOFFELN
kartoffeln
some Potatoes

SPINAT
shpeenaat
some Spinach

TOMATEN
tomaaten
some Tomatoes

APRIKASCHOTEN
aprika shoaten
ome Peppers

RETTICHE
rettisha
some Radishes

ROSENKOHL
rozen coal
some Sprouts

eine TÜTE
eye-na tuwta
a Bag

Groceries — *Lebensmittel*

in *English* order

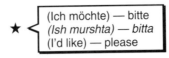
★ (Ich möchte) — bitte
(Ish murshta) — bitta
(I'd like) — please

BIER
beer
some Beer

ÖL
url
some Oil

KEKSE
kekza
some Biscuits/Cookies

ZUCKER
tsookka
some Sugar

BUTTER
bootta
some Butter

TEE
tay
some Tea

KÄSE
kayza
some Cheese

TOILETTENPAPIER
*twal**letten** pap**peer***
some Toilet Paper

KAFFEE
*kaf**fay***
some Coffee

WASCHMITTEL
vash mittle
some Soap Powder

EIER
***eye**-er*
some Eggs

WASSER
vassa
some Water

FRUCHTSAFT
frookht zaft
some Fruit Juice

(ROT/WEIß) WEIN
(rote/vice) vine
(red/white) Wine

HONIG
***hoa**nish*
some Honey

JOGHURT
***yoh**goort*
some Yogurt

 MARMELADE
*marma**laa**da*
some Jam

MARGARINE
*margha-**ree**na*
some Margarine

**(VOLL/FETTARME)
MILCH**
*(foll/**fett**arma) milsh*
(whole/skimmed) Milk

 Salz
zalts
salt

 Pfeffer
*p**feff**a*
Pepper

32

Kleidung — *Kly-doong* — Clothes

eine Mütze
eye-na muwtza
a Woolly Hat

eine Unterhose
eye-na oonterhoza
some Underpants/Briefs

einen Badeanzug
***eye**-nen baada **ant**zoog*
a Swimming Costume

einen Hut
***eye**-nen hoot*
a Hat

einen Rock
***eye**-nen rock*
a Skirt

ein Hemd/eine Bluse
ine hemt/eye-na blooza
a Shirt/Blouse

ein Kleid
ine klite
a Dress

einen Regenmantel
***eye**-nen **ray**ghen mantle*
a Raincoat

eine Hose
eye-na hoza
some Trousers

eine Strumpfhose
*eye-na sh**trumpf**hoza*
some Tights

Socken
***zock**en*
some Socks

Handschuhe
***hant** shoe-a*
some Gloves

einen Pullover
***eye**-nen **pull**over*
a Sweater

ein Paar Schuhe/Sandalen
*ine par shoe-a/zan**daal**en*
a Pair of Shoes/Sandals

einen Gürtel
***eye**-nen **guwr**tel*
a belt

Shorts
shorts
some Shorts

ein Taschentuch
*ine **tash**entookh*
a Handkerchief

Buying Clothes

1. *Gooten taag, bitta **shurn**?*
   Hallo, can I help you?
3. *Velsha grursa?*
   What size?
5. ***Haa**ben zee deeza art in bl-ow?*
   Have you got this one in blue?

2. *Ish murshta gairna **eye**-nen **pull**over **cow**-fen.*
   I'd like to buy a pullover.
4. *Ish haaba grursa **feert**-sish.*
   ***Kurn**ten zee meer **mass nay**men?*
   I take size 40.
   Can you measure me?

1. *Vo ist dee **an**proba?*
   Where is the fitting room?
3. *Ess past nisht.*
   It doesn't fit me.

2. *Ess past zayr goot.*
   It fits very well.
4. *Ess ist tsoo groce/klyne.*
   It's too big/small.
5. *Ess ist tsoo **toy**-er.*
   It's too dear.

Methods of Payment

> 1. Es gefällt mir. Das nehme ich. Was kostet das?
>
> 3. Nehmen Sie Kreditkarten/Dollar/Eurocheques/Reiseschecks?
>
> 4. Danke schön.
>
> 2. Bitte an der Kasse bezahlen.
>
> 5. Nichts zu danken.
>
> KASSE

1. *Ess ghe-**felt** meer. Dass nayma ish. Vass **kostet** dass?*
   I like it. I'll take it.
   How much is it?

3. ***Nay**men zee kre**deet**karten/**doll**aar/**oy**roshecks/ryza-shecks?*
   Do you take credit cards/dollars/Eurocheques/traveller's cheques?

2. *Bitta an dair kassa bet**zaal**en.*
   Please pay at the cash desk.

4. *Danka shurn.*
   Thank you very much.

5. *Nishts tsoo **dank**en.*
   Not at all.

Apotheke — *Appotayka* — Chemist/Drugstore

An Apotheke mostly sells drugs and medicines. For health foods try also the Reformhaus. Toiletries are sold in the Drogerie (see p.36).

Haben Sie etwas gegen —?
***Haab**en zee **et**vass **gay**ghen —*
Have you anything for —?

Seekrankheit
***zay**krank-hite*
Seasickness

Verstopfung
*fair-**shtopf**oong*
Constipation

Heuschnupfen
***hoy**-shnupfen*
Hay fever

Sonnenbrand
***zonn**enbrant*
Sunburn

Husten
***hoos**ten*
a Cough

Ohrenschmerzen
***ohr**en sh**mairt**sen*
Earache

Insektenstiche
*in**zek**ten-shtisha*
Insect bites

Durchfall
***doysh**fal*
Diarrhoea

Magenschmerzen
***maa**ghen sh**mairt**sen*
Stomach Ache

Kopfschmerzen
***kopf** sh**mairt**sen*
a Headache

Halsschmerzen
***halce** sh**mairt**sen*
a Sore Throat

Welche Apotheke hat Nachtdienst (Notdienst)?
*Velsha appo**tay**ka hat nakht deenst (note deenst)?*
Which chemist is on evening (emergency) duty?

(see also Medical Section p.62 and Parts of the Body p.63)

Drogerie — Apotheke
Toiletries — Medicines

— bitte
— *bitta*
— please ★

WATTE
vatta
some Cotton Wool

SONNENKREM
zonnen krame
some Suntan Cream

SHAMPOO
shampoo
some Shampoo

WUNDSALBE
voont zalba
Antiseptic Cream

ASPIRIN
aspireen
some Aspirin

DAMENBINDEN/TAMPONS
daamen **binn**den/**tam**pons
Sanitary/Napkins/Towels/Tampons

PAPIERTASCHENTÜCHER
*papp**eer** tashen**tuw**sher
Paper Handkerchiefs

KONDOME
kon-**dom**a
some Condoms

ein RASIERAPPARAT
ine razzeer appa**raat**
a Razor

(HEFT) PFLASTER
(heft) pflasta
some Sticking Plasters

eine BINDE
eye-na binnda
a Bandage

WINDELN
vinndeln
some Nappies

INSEKTENMITTEL
in**zek**ten **mitt**le
some Insect Repellant

SEIFE
z-**eye**-fa
some Soap

KINDERNAHRUNG/CREME
kinnda **naa**roong/crayma
some Baby Food/Cream

ZAHNPASTA
ts**aan**pasta
some Toothpaste

SONNENBRILLE
zonnen brilla
some Sunglasses

ein KAMM
ine kamm
a Comb

eine ZAHNBÜRSTE

*eye-na ts**aan**-bewrsta*
a Toothbrush

ein DEODORANT
*ine dayodor-**ant***
a Deodorant

SONNENÖL
zonnen url
some Suntan Oil

36

WHO SELLS WHAT

Buchhandlung	Schreibwaren	Zeitschriften
Bookshop	Stationery	Newspapers

ein (Englisch-Deutsch)
WÖRTERBUCH
*ine `(**eng**-lish doytsh)*
***vur**ter bookh*
an (English-German)
Dictionary

ein BUCH
ine bookh
a Book

eine KARTE
eye-na karta
a Map

eine (englische) ZEITUNG
*eye-na (**eng**-lisha) ts-**eye**toong*
an (English) Newspaper

ein FILM
ine film
a film

ein KUGELSCHREIBER
*ine koogle **shry**ber*
a (Ballpoint) Pen

ein BLEISTIFT
*ine **bly**-shtift*
a Pencil

Tabakwaren
Cigarettes and Tobacco

eine BRIEFMARKE
*eye-na **brief**marka*
a Stamp

eye-na posst karta
eine POSTKARTE
a Postcard

STREICHHÖLZER
*sh-**trysh** hurltser*
some Matches

ein FEUERZEUG
ine foya tsoyg
a Lighter

NÄHGARN
***nay**garn*
some Thread

(Filter) ZIGARETTEN
*(filter) tsigga**ret**ten*
(Filter) Cigarettes

eine NÄHNADEL
*eye-na **nay**naadel*
a Needle

ein FLASCHENÖFFNER
*ine **flash**en urfner*
a Bottle Opener

Eisenwarenhändler
Ironmonger

ein BÜCHSENÖFFNER
*ine **buwkh**sen urfner*
a Tin/Can Opener

eine GASFLASCHE
eye-na Gas flasha
a Camping Gaz Bottle

eine TASCHENLAMPE
*eye-na **tash**en lampa*
a Torch/Flashlight

eine BATTERIE
*eye-na batte**ree***
a Battery

ein KORKENZIEHER
*ine **kork**ent **zee**-er*
a Corkscrew

eine SCHERE
*eye-na **shay**-ra*
some Scissors

BINDFADEN
***bint**faaden*
some String

eine LEINE
eye-na lyna
Cord, Rope

ein KÜHL-ELEMENT
ine Kuwl Element
an Ice Pack

37

BANKS

You can change
money at banks
like these or at
major post
offices —

BANKING HOURS are 8.30 a.m. to 1.00 p.m. and 2.30
p.m. to 4.00 p.m. Mondays to Fridays (Thursdays 5.30
p.m.), with slight regional variations.

Public Holidays — *Feiertage*

D	New Year	January 1	A	CH
		January 2		CH
	Epiphany	January 6	A	
D	Good Friday	March/		CH
D	Easter Monday	April	A	CH
D	May Day	May 1	A	
D	Ascension	May	A	CH
D	Whit Monday	May/June	A	CH
	Corpus Christi	June	A	
D	Nat. Unity Day	June 17		
	National Day	August 1		CH
	Assumption	August 15	A	
	National Day	October 26	A	
	All Saints' Day	November 1	A	
D	Christmas Day	December 25	A	CH
D	Boxing Day	December 26	A	CH

Plus local holidays

D—Germany   A—Austria   CH—Switzerland

1a. Bitte, wo kann ich hier Geld wechseln?

1b. Entschuldigen Sie bitte, wo ist die nächste Bank?

2. Da drüben, am Marktplatz.

BANK — EXCHANGE BUREAU

Bank
Wechselstube
Geldwechsel

bank
vexel shtooba
ghelt vexel

Look for any of these words if you want to change money or traveller's cheques.

Exchange bureaux at main railway stations and airports open later but charge slightly more.

1a. *Bitta, vo can ish here ghelt vexelln?*
Where can I change some money, please?

1b. *Entshooldiggen zee bitta, vo ist dee nekhsta bank?*
Excuse me, where is the nearest bank?

2. *Da drewben, am markt plats.*
Over there in the market place.

Geld	Kleingeld	Münze	Münz/Geldwechsler
ghelt	*kline ghelt*	*muwntsa*	*muwnts/ghelt veksla*
money	small change	coin	coin changer

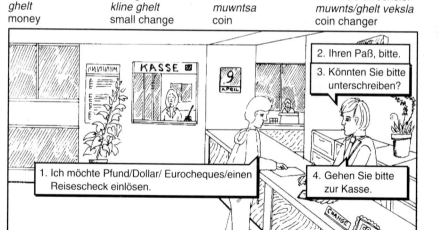

2. Ihren Paß, bitte.

3. Könnten Sie bitte unterschreiben?

1. Ich möchte Pfund/Dollar/ Eurocheques/einen Reisescheck einlösen.

4. Gehen Sie bitte zur Kasse.

1. *Ish murshta pfoont/dollaar/ oyroshecks/eye-nen ryza-sheck ine-lursen.*
I'd like to change some pounds/ dollars/Eurocheques/ a travellers' cheque.

2. *Eeren pass, bitta.*
Your passport, please.

3. *Kurnten zee bitta oonta-shryben?*
Please sign here.

4. *Gay-en zee bitta tsoor kassa.*
Please go to the cashier.

Post Office — Post, Postamt

Vo ist dee posst, bitta?
Where is the post office, please?

Buying Stamps — Briefmarken

1. Eine Briefmarke für diesen Brief (diese Postkarte), bitte.
2. Nach Großbritannien, bitte.

Stamps: Look in the Post Office for the sign **(Post) wertzeichen** or **Briefmarken (kl. Mengen** means small amounts).

Most shops selling post-cards also sell stamps.

Many post offices change **money** and cash euro-cheques: look for the **ec** symbol.

1. *Eye-na **brief**marka fewr **dee**zen brief (deeza **posst**karta) bitta.*
    Could I have a stamp for this letter (postcard), please.

2. *Nakh Groce Brit**taan**yen, bitta.*
    To Great Britain, please.

Telephone — *Telefon* (taylayfone)

Wo kann ich hier telefonieren? ★

*Vo can ish here telefonn-**eeren**?*
Where can I make a 'phone call?

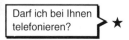

Inland und Ausland

Öffentlicher Fernsprecher
Public Telephone

Darf ich bei Ihnen telefonieren? ★

*Darf ish by **een**en telefonn-**eeren**?*
May I use your 'phone, please?

You can also make long-distance calls from post offices (pay afterwards).
Look for this sign: **FERNGESPRÄCHE.**

Notruf: Emergency: dial 110
(Fire Brigade 112). You need 3 x 10-Pfennig coins unless it says **Kein Geld ...** or **Münzfreier Notruf.**

Directory enquiries: 11 88 (inland)
001 18 (international)

RINGING HOME: You can ring direct from all call boxes (except those marked **Inland** or **National**).

AUSLAND or **INTERNATIONAL** = abroad (**Gespräche** = calls).

Dial 00 then your country code, followed by the code for your town (leave off the first 0)

Britain .... dial 00 then   44
U.S. and Canada .... dial 00 then   1
Australia .... dial 00 then   61
New Zealand .... dial 00 then   64
Eire .... dial 00 then 353

3. Kann ich Herrn (Frau), — sprechen?

FERNGESPRÄCHE

1. Ich möchte nach Köln telefonieren.

2. Ich möchte ein R-Gespräch anmelden. ★

1. *Ish murshta nakh Kurln telefonn-**eeren**.*
I want to ring Cologne.

2. *Ish murshta ine air- gush**praysh** an**melden**.*
I'd like to make a reverse-charge (collect) call.

3. *Can ish **Hair**en (Fr-ow),— sh**prekh**en?*
May I speak to Mr. (Mrs.),— please?

RUF MAL AN!   Give me a ring!

die Stadt
dee shtatt
the town

★ Bitte, wie komme ich nach – ?

Bitta, vee comma ish nakh – ?
How do I get to – please?

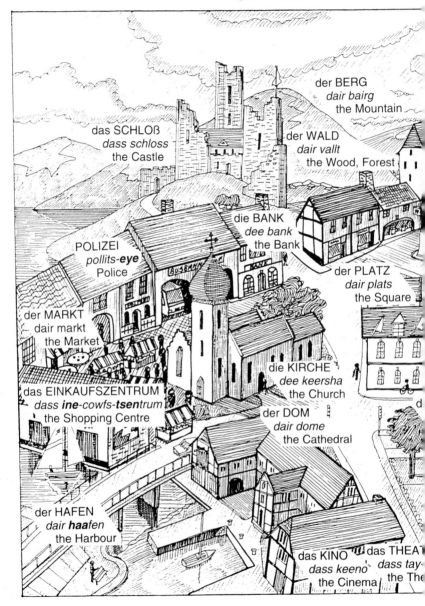

der BERG
dair bairg
the Mountain

das SCHLOß
dass schloss
the Castle

der WALD
dair vallt
the Wood, Forest

die BANK
dee bank
the Bank

POLIZEI
pollits-eye
Police

der PLATZ
dair plats
the Square

der MARKT
dair markt
the Market

die KIRCHE
dee keersha
the Church

das EINKAUFSZENTRUM
dass ine-cowfs-tsentrum
the Shopping Centre

der DOM
dair dome
the Cathedral

der HAFEN
dair haafen
the Harbour

das KINO
dass keeno
the Cinema

das THEA
dass tay
the The

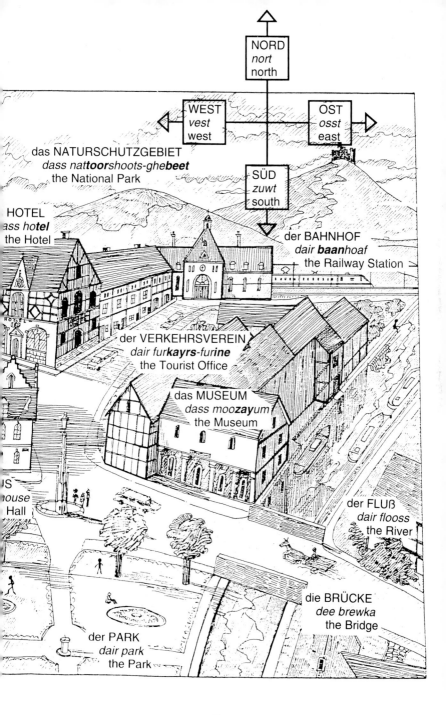

NORD
nort
north

WEST
vest
west

OST
osst
east

SÜD
zuwt
south

das NATURSCHUTZGEBIET
dass nattoorshoots-ghebeet
the National Park

HOTEL
ass hotel
the Hotel

der BAHNHOF
dair baanhoaf
the Railway Station

der VERKEHRSVEREIN
dair furkayrs-furine
the Tourist Office

das MUSEUM
dass moozayum
the Museum

der FLUß
dair flooss
the River

US
ouse
Hall

der PARK
dair park
the Park

die BRÜCKE
dee brewka
the Bridge

Finding the way

Wo ist?
Vo ist?
Where is?

1. Bitte, wo ist die Parkstraße?
2. Hier geradeaus und dann die erste Straße rechts.
3. Bitte, zeigen Sie mir das auf der Karte.
4. Ist das weit?

1. *Bitta, vo ist dee Park Shtraasa?*
   Excuse me, where is Park Street?

2. *Here gheraada-owss oont dan dee airsta shtraasa rekhts.*
   Straight ahead and then first right.

3. *Bitta, **tsy**-ghen zee meer dass owf dair karta.*
   Could you show me on the map, please?

4. *Ist dass vyte?*
   Is it far?

hier, dort
here, dort
here, there

bis zu
biss tsoo
as far as

gegenüber
***gay**ghen-uwba*
opposite

die Kreuzung
*dee **kroyt**zoong*
the crossroads

an der Ecke
an dair ekka
on the corner

neben
***nay**ben*
next to

die Verkehrsampel
*dee fur-**kayr**zample*
the traffic lights

geradeaus
*gheraada-**owss***
straight on

nach links
nakh links
to the left

nach rechts
nakh rekhts
to the right

hinter
hinter
behind

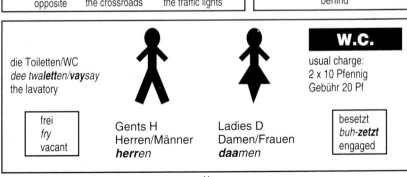

die Toiletten/WC
*dee twa**letten**/**vay**say*
the lavatory

frei
fry
vacant

Gents H
Herren/Männer
***herr**en*

Ladies D
Damen/Frauen
***daa**men*

W.C.

usual charge:
2 x 10 Pfennig
Gebühr 20 Pf

besetzt
*buh-**zetzt***
engaged

Road Travel

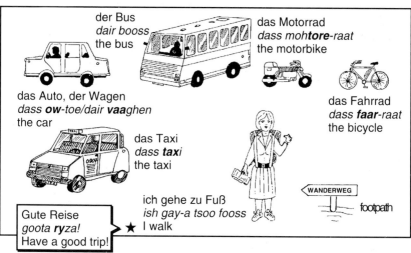

der Bus
dair booss
the bus

das Motorrad
dass mohtore-raat
the motorbike

das Auto, der Wagen
dass ow-toe/dair vaaghen
the car

das Fahrrad
dass faar-raat
the bicycle

das Taxi
dass taxi
the taxi

ich gehe zu Fuß
ish gay-a tsoo fooss
I walk

WANDERWEG footpath

Gute Reise
goota ryza!
Have a good trip!

Round road signs tell you to do or not to do something. Square or oblong signs give information and triangular ones warn you of danger.

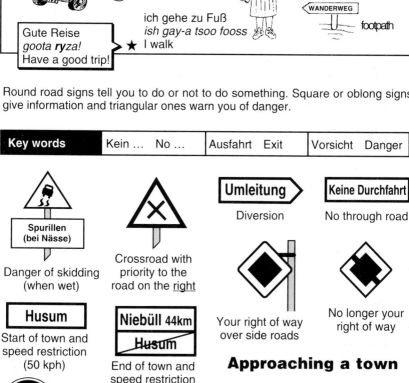

| Key words | Kein … No … | Ausfahrt Exit | Vorsicht Danger |

Spurillen
(bei Nässe)

Danger of skidding
(when wet)

Crossroad with
priority to the
road on the <u>right</u>

Umleitung
Diversion

Keine Durchfahrt
No through road

Husum
Start of town and
speed restriction
(50 kph)

Niebüll 44km
Husum
End of town and
speed restriction

Your right of way
over side roads

No longer your
right of way

Approaching a town

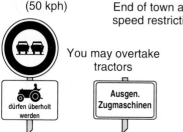

You may overtake
tractors

dürfen überholt
werden

Ausgen.
Zugmaschinen

Get in Lane
Einordnen

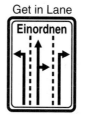

Stadtmitte
Town Centre

In town — Stadtmitte, Innenstadt, Zentrum

N.B. Pedestrians <u>must</u> wait for the green man when crossing the road at traffic lights

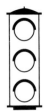

Stadtteil
district

Industrie (Gewerbe) gebiet
industrial estate

Einbahnstraße
One-way street

Anlieger frei
or **Anliegerverkehr**
Access for residents only

gesperrt
closed to traffic

Fußgängerzone
Pedestrian zone

Durchgang verboten!
No access

Ausfahrt freihalten
Keep clear

To park (or not to park)

Bitte nicht parken!   **Parken verboten**
No parking

Nur für PKW (LKW) only for cars (lorries)

P

PARK IN ANY OF THESE: **Parkgarage, Parkhaus, Tiefgarage**
besetzt: full   **frei:** spaces

Parkplätze nur für Kurzparker
Short-term parking only

Parking disc needed
(from tobacconists or newsagents)

Parkgebühr (1 Stunde/Std.)
parking fee (1 hour/hr.)

P̂
Undercover parking

Eingang Kasse
to cash desk

Expressway/Motorway — Autobahn *(Ow-toe baan)*

⇐ **Autobahn**

to the motorway

Nicht schneller als
130

maximum speed

Autobahnkreuz

motorways cross

Autobahndreieck

motorways merge

Stau

Traffic jam

Ausfahrt

Exit

Rastplatz
bitte sauber halten

lay-by (please keep clean)

Rasthof **Raststätte**

service area

Tankstelle

petrol station (see p.48)

Licht einschalten

turn on lights

(Bundes) **Grenze**

(German) Frontier

Zoll
Douane

Customs

Breakdown — Emergency — Notruf

Look for orange emergency phone **(Notruf)**
Instructions:
Lift flap and hold.
Wait till motorway control point replies.

(Breakdowns p.49, lower picture)
(Medical p.60)

Gas/Petrol Station — Tankstelle

Bitta, vo ist dee nekhsta **tank**-shtella?
Where is the nearest filling station,
please?

German	Pronunciation / English	German	Pronunciation / English
Benzin	*ben-**tseen***	Normal (benzin)	*nor-**maal** (ben-**tseen**)*
petrol/gas		2-star	
Super	***zoo**per*	Diesel	***dee**zel*
4-star		diesel	
2-Takt Mix	*tsv-**eye** takt mix*	Bleifrei	*bly fry*
2-stroke		lead-free	
Luft	*looft*	Öl	*url*
air		oil	
Wasser	***vass**er*		
water			

> *sb-tanken/selbst tanken*
> self-service

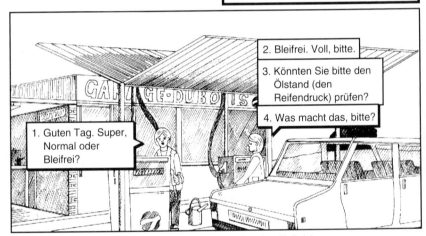

2. Bleifrei. Voll, bitte.

3. Könnten Sie bitte den Ölstand (den Reifendruck) prüfen?

4. Was macht das, bitte?

1. Guten Tag. Super, Normal oder Bleifrei?

1. ***Goo**ten taag. **Zoo**per, nor-**maal**, oda bly fry?*
   Hello. 4-star, 2-star or lead-free?

3. ***Kurn**ten zee bitta dane **url**-shtant (dane **ry**fen-drook) **pruw**fen?*
   Please check the oil (tyre pressure).

2. *Bly fry. Foll, bitta,*
   Lead-free. Fill it up, please.

4. *Vass makht dass, bitta?*
   How much is that?

> Reifendienst
> Tyre service

Beleg entnehmen. An der Kasse bezahlen
Take bill and pay at cash desk

Benzin on the pump refers to Normal/2-star petrol.

Breakdowns and Repairs

1. Ich habe eine Panne.
   Könnten Sie mir helfen?

2. Darf ich bei Ihnen telefonieren?

3. Wo ist eine Reparaturwerkstatt?

PGB 678

1. *Ish haaba eye-na panna.* **Kurn**ten zee meer **helf**en?
   I have broken down.
   Can you help me, please?

2. *Darf ish by **een**en* telefonn-**eer**en?
   May I use your phone?

3. *Vo ist eye-na reparrat**toor-vairk**shtatt?*
   Where is there a garage?

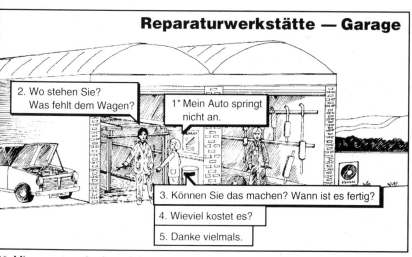

Reparaturwerkstätte — Garage

2. Wo stehen Sie?
   Was fehlt dem Wagen?

1* Mein Auto springt nicht an.

3. Können Sie das machen? Wann ist es fertig?

4. Wieviel kostet es?

5. Danke vielmals.

1*. *Mine **ow**-toe shpringt nisht an.*
   My car won't start.

3. **Kurn**en zee dass **makh**en?
   Van ist ess **fair**tish?
   Can you repair it?
   How long will it take?

5. *Danka **feel**malss.*
   Thank you very much.

2. *Vo **shtay**en zee?*
   Vass faylt dame **vaa**ghen?
   Where are you?
   What's the matter with the car?

4. *Veefeel **kost**et ess?*
   What do I owe you?

*For a selection of car components and things that might go wrong, see next page.

On Two and Four Wheels

Ich brauche —
Ish browsha —
I need —

Der Motor setzt plötzlich aus.
Dair mohtore zetzt plurtslish owss.
The engine is stalling.

*ist nicht in Ordnung.
**ist nisht in ordnoong.*
*isn't working.

Der Motor läuft sich heiß.
Dair mohtore loyft zish hice.
The engine is overheating.

Car, Bicycle and Motorcycle parts (in *English*) order

1. der Luftfilter
   dair looft filter
   the Air Filter

2. die Batterie
   dee batteree
   the Battery

3. die Bremsen
   dee bremzen
   the Brakes

4. die Bremsschuhe
   dee bremss shoe·a
   the Brake Blocks

5. eine Birne
   eye-na beerna
   a Bulb

6. das Kabel
   dass kaable
   the Cable

7. der Vergaser
   dair fairgaaza
   the Carburettor

8. die Kette
   dee ketta
   the Chain

9. die Starterklappe
   dee shtarter klappa
   the Choke

10. die Kupplung
    dee kooploong
    the Clutch

11. der Verteiler
    dair fair-tyler
    the Distributor

12. die Elektrische Ausrüstung
    elecktrisha owsruwstoong
    the Electrical System

13. der Motor
    dair mohtore
    the Engine

14. der Auspuff
    dair owsspoof
    the Exhaust

15. der Keilriemen
    dair kyle-reemen
    the Fan Belt

16. die Vordergabel
    dee forder-gaable
    the Front Fork

17. eine Sicherung
    eye-na zisheroong
    a Fuse

18. eine Dichtung
    eye-na dishtoong
    a Gasket

19. Gang (Schaltung)
    gang (shaltoong)
    Gear (Change)

20. die Lenkstange
    dee lenk-shtanga
    the Handlebars

21. der Scheinwerfer
    dair shine-vairfa
    the Headlight

22. ein Schlauch
    ine shl-owkh
    an Inner Tube

23. der Schlüssel
    dair shluwsel
    the Key

24. ein Ölleck/Wasserleck
    ine url/vasser leck
    an Oil/Water Leak

25. das Licht
    dass lisht
    the Light
26. der Gepäckträger
    dair ghepeck-trayger
    the Luggage Carrier
27. eine Gepäckspinne
    eye-na ghepeck-shpinna
    a Luggage Elastic
28. ein Schutzblech
    ine shoots-blesh
    a Mudguard
29. eine Schraubenmutter
    eye-na shr-owbenmutter
    a Nut
30. ein Benzinkanister
    ine bentseen kanister
    a Petrol Can
31. die Unterbrecherkontakte
    oonterbresher kontakta
    the Points
32. die Luftpumpe
    dee looft poompa
    the Pump
33. der Kühler
    dair kuwler
    the Radiator
34. die Satteltasche
    dee zattle tasha
    the Saddlebag
35. eine Schraube
    eye-na shr-owba
    a Screw, Bolt
36. ein Schraubenzieher
    ine shr-owbentzee-a
    a Screwdriver
37. ein Stoßdämpfer
    ine shtoss-dempfer
    a Shock Absorber
38. der Auspufftopf
    dair owspoof-topf
    the Silencer
39. ein Schlüssel
    ine shluwsel
    a Spanner
40. eine Zündkerze
    eye-na tsuwnt kairtsa
    a Sparking Plug
41. die Speichen
    dee shpyshen
    the Spokes

42. ein Reifen
    ine ryfen
    a Tyre
43. der Reifendruck
    dair ryfen-drook
    the Tyre Pressure
44. ein Ventil
    ine venteel
    a Valve
45. ein Rad
    ine raat
    a Wheel
46. die Windschutzscheibe
    dee vintshoots-shyba
    the Windscreen/shield
47. der Scheibenwischer
    dair shyben visha
    the Windscreen Wiper

ein Sturzhelm
ine shtoorts helm
a Crash Helmet

eine Reifenpanne
eye-na ryfen-panna
a Puncture/Flat

Schneeketten
shnay ketten
Snow Chains

Fahrrad-Verleih
Bicycle Hire

Fahrrad am Bahnhof
Many German railway stations have bikes for
hire (half price if you arrive by train)

Car Hire — Autovermietung

1. *Gooten taag. Ish murshta ine ow-toe meeten.*
   Hallo. I'd like to hire a car.

2. *Vass fewr ine ow-toe — ine klynas, mitleress, grocers?*
   What sort of car — small, medium, large?

1. *Fewr vee langa? Fewr eye-nen taag, eye-na vokha?*
   How long for?
   For one day, one week?

2. *Veefeel kostet ess? Veefeel mooss ish hinter-layghen?*
   What is the rate?
   How much is the deposit?

3. *Ist ess murglish, dass ow-toe in Muwnshen zuruwk-tsoo-gayben?*
   May I leave the car in Munich?

4. *Here ist mine fuwrershine.*
   Here is my driving licence.

Buying Tickets: Basic Pattern

2. Einfache Fahrt oder hin und zurück?

1. Einmal (zweimal) Hamburg, bitte.

3. Hin und zurück. Was kostet das, bitte?

4. Ich möchte eine Platzkarte (Liegewagenkarte/Schlafwagenkarte).

Wohin fahren Sie?
Vohin faaren zee?
Where are you going?

Ich fahre nach —
Ish faara nakh —
I'm going to —

erste/zweite Klasse
airsta/tsv-eyeta klassa
1st/2nd class

Raucher oder Nichtraucher?
R-owkha oda...
Smoker or non-smoker

1. ***Ine*-mal *(tsv-eye-mal)* *Ham*boorg, bitta.**
   One (two) to Hamburg, please.

2. ***Ine*-fakha faart oda hin oont zuruwk?**
   Single or return?

3. *Hin oont zuruwk. Vass kostet dass, bitta?*
   Return/round trip. How much is that, please?

4. *Ish murshta eye-na platskarta (leegavaaghen-karta/ shlaaf-vaaghen-karta).*
   I'd like to reserve a seat (couchette/sleeper).

1. *Fon velshem glice fairt dair tsoog nakh Bairleen?*
   Which platform does the Berlin train go from?

2. *Fon glice dry.*
   From platform 3.

3. *Van fairt dair (nekhsta) tsoog?*
   When does the (next) train go?

letzte – *letsta*
last

Finding a seat and Local Travel p.56.

2. Von Gleis drei.

1. Von welchem Gleis fährt der Zug nach Berlin?

3. Wann fährt der (nächste) Zug?

Rail Travel

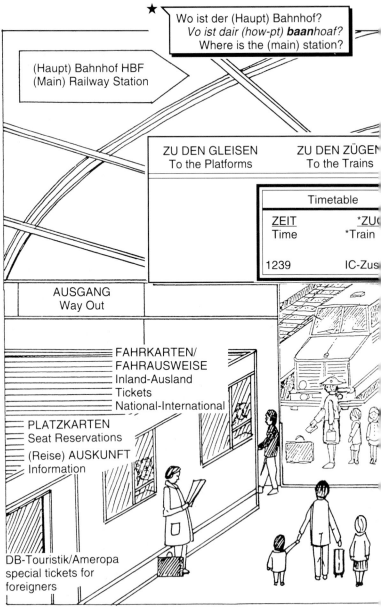

Wo ist der (Haupt) Bahnhof?
*Vo ist dair (how-pt) **baan**hoaf?*
Where is the (main) station?

(Haupt) Bahnhof HBF
(Main) Railway Station

ZU DEN GLEISEN
To the Platforms

ZU DEN ZÜGEN
To the Trains

Timetable

ZEIT	*ZUG
Time	*Train
1239	IC-Zus

AUSGANG
Way Out

FAHRKARTEN/
FAHRAUSWEISE
Inland-Ausland
Tickets
National-International

PLATZKARTEN
Seat Reservations

(Reise) AUSKUNFT
Information

DB-Touristik/Ameropa
special tickets for
foreigners

*Types of Train:
EC (EuroCity) and **IC** (Intercity) are expresses which require a supple
(Zuschlag). **FD, D** and **E** — fast trains. **N** — local train.

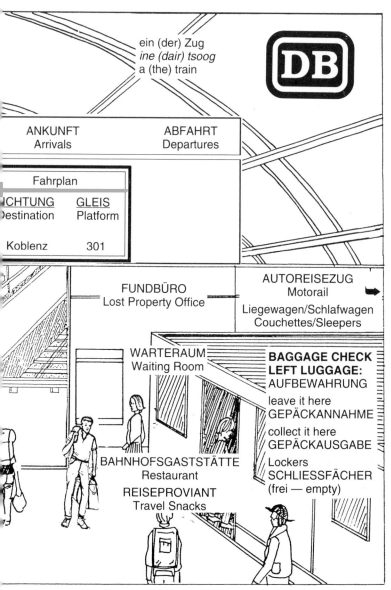

ein (der) Zug
ine (dair) tsoog
a (the) train

DB

ANKUNFT	ABFAHRT
Arrivals	Departures

Fahrplan

ICHTUNG	GLEIS
Destination	Platform
Koblenz	301

FUNDBÜRO
Lost Property Office

AUTOREISEZUG
Motorail
Liegewagen/Schlafwagen
Couchettes/Sleepers

WARTERAUM
Waiting Room

BAHNHOFSGASTSTÄTTE
Restaurant

REISEPROVIANT
Travel Snacks

BAGGAGE CHECK
LEFT LUGGAGE:
AUFBEWAHRUNG

leave it here
GEPÄCKANNAHME

collect it here
GEPÄCKAUSGABE

Lockers
SCHLIESSFÄCHER
(frei — empty)

TABLES: **täglich außer** = daily except: **1-6** Monday-Saturday; **7** Sunday
U — Umsteigen: change   **Kurswagen:** through carriage
Werktags: on weekdays   **Feiertage:** holidays

Finding a seat

RAUCHEN VERBOTEN

No smoking

*Use this phrase to ask for a seat anywhere — bus, plane, park bench, theatre, etc.

1. *Ist deeza plats fry?*
   Is this seat free?
2. *Dass ist mine plats.*
   That's my seat.
3. *Ist dass dair tsoog nakh Veen?*
   Is this the train for Vienna?

Local Transport:

Ticket machines: *Fahrpreis wählen:* choose fare
Geld einwerfen: put in money
Fahrkarte entnehmen: take ticket
Cancelling tickets: see next page.

S-Bahn = Suburban Railway

U-Bahn = Underground/ Subway

Ine-mal **Tem**pelhoaf, bitta.
   One to Tempelhof, please.

1. *Vee komma ish nakh —?*
   How do I get to —?

2. *Leenya feer biss —*
   Line 4 to —.

3. *Mooss ish oomshteye-ghen?*
   Do I have to change?

Buses and Trams

1. Wann fährt der Bus nach Mainz?

2. Wo hält der Bus nach Worms?

3. Welcher Bus fährt in die Stadtmitte?

Haltestelle =
bus stop

Tickets: You can usually use your ticket on all means of transport within a town. Buy it from a machine at the stop. It is often cheaper to buy a booklet of tickets *(Mehrfahrtenkarte). Einzelfahrkarte–* single ticket

1. *Van fairt dair booss nakh **Mine**-ts?*
   What time is the bus for Mainz?

2. *Vo helt dair booss nakh Vormss?*
   Where does the bus for Worms stop?

3. *Velsha booss fairt in dee shtatt-**mitt**a?*
   Which bus goes to the town centre?

 = tram stop

Cancel your ticket in the box marked E *(Entwerter)* or *abstempeln.*

Get **On:** **Ein**stieg
Get **Off:** **Aus**stieg
Richtung — direction

1. Fahren Sie nach Bonn?

2. Ist das der (Haupt) Bahnhof?

1. ***Faa**ren zee nakh Bonn?*
   Do you go to Bonn?

2. *Ist dass dair (how-pt) **baan**hoaf?*
   Is this the (main) station?

Air Travel

1. Wie komme ich zum Flughafen?

1. *Vee komma ish tsoom **floog**haafen?*
   How do I get to the airport?

das Flugzeug
   *dass **floo**gtsoyg*
      the aeroplane

der Flug
   dair floog
      the flight

2. Wann ist der nächste Flug nach Genf?

4. Wann muß ich dort sein?

5. Welche Flugnummer ist es?

3. Um 9 Uhr 10.

2. *Van ist dair nekhsta floog nakh Ghenf?*
      When is the next flight to Geneva?

4. *Van mooss ish dort zine?*
      What time is check in?

3. *Oom noyn oor tsayn.*
      At 9.10.

5. *Velsha **floog**numma ist ess?*
      What is the flight number?

1. Ich möchte diesen Flug umbuchen annullieren).

2. Bitte für Montag einen Flug nach London.

1. *Ish murshta **dee**zen floog **oom**bookhen (annoo**leer**en).*
      I'd like to change (cancel) my reservation on this flight.

2. *Bitta fewr **moan**taag **eye**-nen floog nakh **Lonn**-donn.*
      Please could you book me a flight to London for Monday.

58

Boats

← Bootverleih Bootsfahrt Rundfahrten
← Boats for hire Boat trip Excursions

Im Hafen
*Im **haafen***
At the harbour

1. Ich möchte ein Boot mieten.

1. *Ish murshta ine boat **mee**ten.*
   I'd like to hire a boat.

2. Für eine (eine halbe) Stunde.

2. *Fewr eye-na (eye-na halba) shtoonda.*
   For one (half an) hour.

1. *Van fairt dass shiff nakh **Hel**golant?*
   When does the boat to Heligoland go?

2. *Vo?*
   Where?

3. *Vee langa **dow**-ert dee **uw**berfaart?*
   How long does the crossing take?

GEFAHR
DANGER

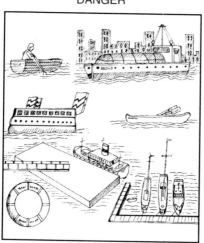

die Fähre
dee fayra
the Ferry

die Insel
*dee **in**zel*
the Island

der See
dair zay
the Lake

ein Rettungsring
*ine **rett**oongssring*
a Lifebelt

das Rettungsboot
*dass **rett**oongssboat*
the Lifeboat

der Kai
dair k-eye
the Quay

die See
dee zay
the Sea

ein Motorboot
ine mohtore-boat
a Motorboat

Tretboot
***tret**boat*
Pedalo

Ruderboot
***roo**derboat*
Rowing boat

Schlauchboot
*shl-**ow**kh boat*
Rubber Dinghy

Segelboot
***zay**ghel boat*
Yacht

Accidents and Illness

Krankenhaus/Klinik Hospital	Notfälle/Ambulanz Casualty Department	Feuerwehr Fire Brigade

FIRST AID
look for:

> *Sanitätsstation*
> *Unfallhilfsstelle*
> *Rettungsdienst*
> *Erste Hilfe*

EMERGENCY
look for:

Notdienst	emergency services
Notarzt *Unfallarzt* }	emergency doctor
Notruf	emergency call

1. Hilfe!
2. Schnell! Rufen Sie einen Krankenwagen.

1. *Hilfa!* Help!	2. *Shnell!* **Roof**en *zee* **eye**-nen **krank**en-**vaa**ghen. Quick! Call an ambulance.

Minor ailments: See Chemist's section page 35.

Calling the doctor/Making an appointment

a. Ich bin krank. Rufen Sie bitte einen `Arzt!

b. Ich möchte gern zu Herrn Doktor. Wann kann ich kommen?

Dr. med. J. Schmidt
prakt. Arzt
doctor of medicine
(*Ärztin* — lady doctor)

Sprechstunden/
Sprechzeiten
consulting hours

nach Vereinbarung
by appointment

Alle Kassen
free treatment
(with Form E111 from
the D.S.S.)

nur privat: private
patients only

a. *Ish bin krank.* **Roof**en *zee bitta* **eye**-nen *artst.*
I'm ill. Please get a doctor.

b. *Ish murshta gairn tsoo* **hair**en **dok**tore. *Van kan ish* **kommen**?
I'd like to see the doctor. When can I come?

At the Doctor's (Parts of the body p.63)

1. *Vo **haab**en zee sh**mairt**sen?*
   Where does it hurt?
2. *Zyte **van** zint zee krank?*
   How long have you been ill?
3. *Here toot ess vay.*
   It hurts here.
4. *Ish haaba **feeb**er.*
   I have a temperature.
5. *Ish haaba mish **uwb**er-**gay**ben.*
   *(Ish bin gush-**tokh**en **vor**den).*
   I've been sick.
   (I've been stung).
6. *Zint zee **gay**ghen tetanus ghe-**imp**ft?*
   Have you been vaccinated
   against tetanus?

1. *Ish nayma **dee**zess medika-**ment** **ray**ghel-**mess**ish.*
   I take this medicine regularly.
2. ***Kur**nen zee meer bitta ine ret**sept gay**ben?*
   Could you give me a prescription, please?
3. *Zee **duwr**fen nisht **ess**en ... **(trink**en).*
   You must not eat ... (drink).
4. *Vee alt ist air (zee)?*
   How old is he (she)?
5. *— yaara.*
   — years old.
6. *Vass bin ish **een**en **shool**dish?*
   How much do I owe you?

When to take your medicine:

äußerlich
for external use
innerlich
for internal use
(drei)mal täglich
(3) times a day
alle — Stunden
every — hours
während — Tagen
for — days
morgens/nachts
in the morning/at night
vor/nach dem Essen
before/after meals
lutschen — suck
schlucken — swallow

98·6°F = 37°C

What the doctor needs to know:

Ich bin … *Ish bin* … I'm …
allergisch gegen
*all**airg**hish **gay**ghen*
allergic to
Asthmatiker
*ast-**maa**tiker*
asthmatic
Diabetiker   Epileptiker
*dee-a**bett**iker   epi**lep**tiker*
diabetic   epileptic
Ich erwarte ein Baby
*Ish air**var**ta ine baby*
I'm pregnant
Ich habe hohen Blutdruck
*Ish haaba **hoe**-en **bloot**drook*
I have high blood pressure
Ich habe einen Herzfehler
*Ish haaba **eye**-nen **hairts**fayla*
I have heart trouble

At the Dentist — Zahnarzt

Dr. Norbert Sandvoss
  Zahnarzt
  2. Etage
(Etage — floor)

1. Ich habe Zahnschmerzen.

2. Ich möchte gern einen Termin
   (so bald wie möglich).

3. Tut es hier weh?

4. Hier tut es weh.

1. *Ish haaba **tsaan**-shmairtsen.*
   I've got toothache.

2. *Ish murshta gairn **eye**-nen tair**meen**
   (zo balt vee **mur**glish).*
   Can I make an appointment
   (as soon as possible)?

3. *Toot ess here vay?*
   Does that hurt?

4. *Hier tut es weh.*
   It hurts here.

Parts of the Body — listed alphabetically

der Knöchel
*dair **knur**schel*
the Ankle

der Arm
dair arrm
the Arm

der Rücken
*dair **ruw**ken*
the Back

die Brust
dee broost
the Chest

das Ohr
dass ohr
the Ear

der Ellbogen
*dair **el**boaghen*
the Elbow

das Auge
*dass **ow**-ga*
the Eye

das Gesicht
*dass ghe**zisht***
the Face

der Finger
dair fing-a
the Finger

der Fuß
dair fooss
the Foot

das Haar
dass har
the Hair

die Hand
dee hant
the Hand

der Kopf
dair koppf
the Head

das Herz
dass hairts
the Heart

der Körper
*dair **kur**per*
The Body

Hier tut es weh
Here toot ess vay
It hurts here

★

das Knie
*dass k-**nee***
the Knee

das Bein
dass bine
the Leg

der Mund
dair moont
the Mouth

der Hals
dair halss
the Neck

die Nase
dee naaza
the Nose

der Magen
*dair **maa**ghen*
the Stomach

die Haut
dee how-t
the Skin

die Zähne
dee tsayna
the Teeth

der Hals
dair halss
the Throat

die Zunge
dee tsung-a
the Tongue

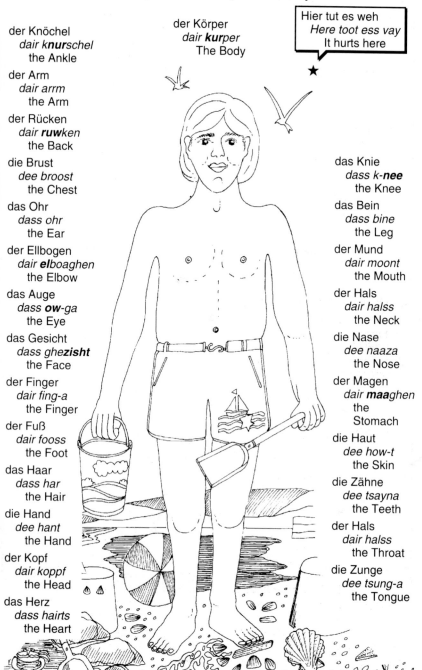

63

Sport

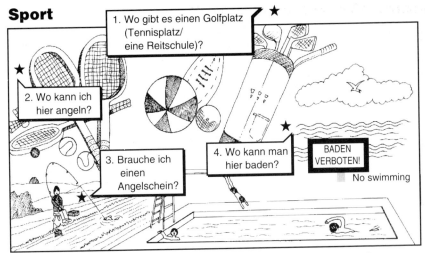

1. *Vo gibt ess **eye**-nen golf plats
   (ten**niss** plats/ **eye**-na rite shoola)?*
   Where is there a golf course
   (tennis court/riding school)?

3. *Brow-kha ish **eye**-nen **ang**-ell shine?*
   Do I need a permit?

2. *Vo can ish here **ang**-eln?*
   Where can you go fishing?

4. *Vo can man here **baa**den?*
   Where can you go swimming?

Skiing

1. *Can ish shee **shtoon**den **nay**men?*
   Can I have some skiing
   lessons?

3. *Can ish eye-na shee
   ows**ruwst**oong here **lie**-en?*
   Can I hire some skiing
   equipment?

2. *Yah, gairn.*
   Yes, of course.

4. *Ish brow-kha **eye**-nen shee pass
   (eye-na **taa**gas-karta/**vokh**en-karta)*
   I need a ski pass (a daily/weekly
   pass).

Entertainment: Booking tickets

1. Wann beginnt die Vorstellung?
2. Ich möchte zwei Karten für Samstag.
3. Wie teuer?
4. Etwa für zwanzig Mark.

1. *Van be**gint** dee **for**-shtelloong?*
   When does the performance start?
3. *Vee **toyer**?*
   What price?

2. *Ish murshta tsv-eye **kar**ten fewr **zams**taag.*
   I'd like two tickets for Saturday, please.
4. *Ettva fewr ts**vant**-sish mark.*
   About 20 Marks.

1. Was gibt es heute (morgen abend) im Kino (Theater)?
★
2. Wo kann ich ein Fußballspiel besuchen?
3. Gibt es hier eine Diskothek? ★

1. *Vass gibt ess hoyta (**morgh**en **aab**ent) im keeno (tay**ar**ter)?*
   What's on at the cinema (theatre) today (tomorrow evening)?

2. *Vo can ish ine **fooss**bal-shpeel be**zook**hen?*
   Where can I watch a football match?

3. *Gibt ess here eye-na disco**tekk**?*
   Is there a disco here?

On the piste

1. Ich bin Anfänger.
2. Ich kann gut skilaufen.

der Lift
dair lift
the Ski Lift

die Piste
dee pista
the Ski Run

der Langlauf
*dair **lang**-lowf*
cross-country skiing

die Loipe
dee loypa
the trail

1. *Ish bin **ann**feng-er.*
   I'm a beginner.
2. *Ish can goot shee **lowf**en.*
   I'm good at skiing.

Sightseeing

1. Was kann man in Heidelberg machen?
2. Man kann die Altstadt und das Schloß besichtigen, oder im Wald spazierengehen …
3. Wann wird das Schloß geöffnet?
4. Jeden Tag von vierzehn bis achtzehn Uhr.

EINTRITT	AUSGANG
ine-tritt	*owss*gang
Entrance	Exit

Verboten/Nicht
   Don't!

1. *Vass can man in*
   Hy*del-bairg* **mak***hen?*
      What is there to do in
      Heidelberg?

3. *Van veert dass shloss ghe-***urf***net?*
      When is the castle open?

2. *Man kan dee* **alt***-shtatt*
   *oont dass shloss be***sish***tiggen,*
   *oda im valt shpatt-***zeer***en***gay***en …*
      You can look round the old town
      and the castle, or go for a walk
      in the woods …

4. **Yay***den taag fonn* **feer***-tsayn*
   biss **akht***-tsayn oor.*
      Every day from 2.00-6.00 p.m.

Theft and lost property

1. Ich habe (meinen Paß) verloren.
2. Mir ist (der Paß) gestohlen worden.

1. *Ish haaba (***my***-nen pass)*
   *fair***loren***.*
      I've lost (my passport).

2. *Meer ist (dair pass) ghe-***shtoal***en* **vor***den.*
      My (passport) has been
      stolen.

3. *Vee zaa air owss?*
   *Vass var da-***rin***?*
      What did it look like?
      What was inside?

3. Wie sah er aus?
   Was war darin?

die/meine Tasche	den/meinen Fotoapparat	das/mein Geld
dee/myna tasha	*dane/***my***-nen foto-*	*dass/mine ghelt*
the/my Bag	appa**raat**	the/my Money
	the/my Camera	

Name	Adresse	Wann	Wo	
naama	*ad***dress***a*	*van*	*vo*	}?
Name	Address	When	Where	

Making friends

1. *Gooten taag! Vee gayts?*
   Hallo, how are you?

2. *Danka goot. Oont eenen?*
   Fine thanks — and you?

3. *Ish hy-sa —.*
   Vee hy-sen zee?
   I'm called —.
   What's your name?

4. *Dass ist mine man (myna fr-ow)*
   mine zone (myna tokhta)
   mine froynt (myna froyndin).
   This is my husband (my wife),
   my son (my daughter),
   my friend (male/female).

5. *Zayr airfroyt!*
   Pleased to meet you.

6. *Owf veeda-zane!*
   Goodbye.

1. *Ish hysa —.*
   Vee hy-st doo?
   I'm called —.
   What's your name?

2. *Dass ist mine brooda/*
   myna shvesta.
   This is my brother/my sister.

3. *Hast doo ghe-shvista?*
   Have you any brothers and
   sisters?

4. *Vee alt bist doo?*
   How old are you?

5. *Noyn.*
   Nine.

6. *Chuwss!*
   Goodbye (to children).

Making conversation – or not!

1. Wie gefällt es Ihnen hier?
8. Gehen Sie weg!
3. Woher kommen Sie?
5. Sind Sie zum ersten Mal in Deutschland?
6. Sind Sie schon lange hier?
2. Es gefällt mir sehr gut.
4. Aus Edinburg.
7. Seit einer Woche.

1. *Vee ghe**felt** ess **ee**nen here?*
   How do you like it here?

2. *Ess ghe**felt** meer zayr goot.*
   I like it very much.

3. *Vo**hair komm**en zee?*
   Where do you come from?

4. *Owss **Ed**inboorg.*
   From Edinburgh.

5. *Zint zee tsoom **air**sten mal in **Doyt**shlant?*
   Is this your first visit to Germany?

6. *Zint zee shoan langa here?*
   Have you been here long?

7. *Zyte eye-na vokha.*
   For a week.

8. ***Gay**-en zee vekk!*
   Go away!

Accepting an invitation

1. Haben Sie für heute abend schon etwas vor?
2. Möchten Sie uns (heute abend) besuchen?
3. Das ist sehr nett von Ihnen. Ich komme sehr gern.
4. Wann treffen wir uns?

1. ***Haa**en zee fewr hoyta **aa**bent shoan **et**vass for?*
   Are you free this evening?

2. ***Mur**shten zee oonss (hoyta **aa**bent) be**zoo**khen?*
   Would you like to come and see us (this evening)?

3. *Dass ist zayr net fonn **een**en. Ish komma zayr gairn.*
   That's very nice of you. I'd love to come.

4. *Van **treff**en veer oonss?*
   When shall we meet?

Visiting

1. **Goo**ten taag (aabent)!
   Hairtslish vill**komm**en!
   Good day (evening).
   How nice to see you!

2. Bitta **nay**men zee plats.
   Please sit down.

3. **Mursh**ten zee **et**vass **trink**en?
   Would you like anything to drink?

4. Yah, gairn.
   Yes, please.

5. Vass **makh**en zee in eera **fry**- tsyte?
   What do you do in your spare time?

6. Ish layza oont tantsa gairn,
   ish gay-a gairn shpat-**zeer**en.
   Ish interress-**eer**a mish
   fewr moo**zeek**, shport …
   I like reading and dancing,
   I like walking. I'm interested in music, sport …

7. Hat ess ghe-sh**meckt**?
   Did you like it?

8. Dass var **kurst**lish.
   That was delicious.

Saying goodbye

1. **Feel**en dank fewr
   dane **nett**en **aa**bent.
   Thank you for a
   lovely evening.

2. **Komm**en zee balt
   veeda.
   Come again soon.

3. Owf veeda-zane!
   Goodbye.

My Family — meine Familie — *myna fameelya*

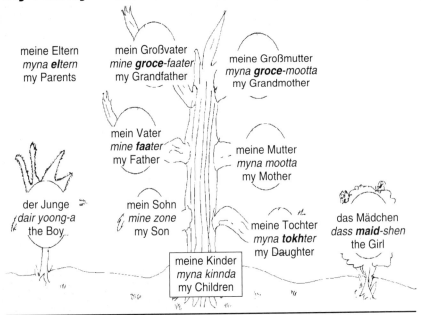

meine Eltern
*myna **eltern***
my Parents

mein Großvater
*mine **groce**-faater*
my Grandfather

meine Großmutter
*myna **groce**-mootta*
my Grandmother

mein Vater
*mine **faa**ter*
my Father

meine Mutter
myna mootta
my Mother

der Junge
dair yoong-a
the Boy

mein Sohn
mine zone
my Son

meine Tochter
*myna **tokh**ter*
my Daughter

das Mädchen
*dass **maid**-shen*
the Girl

meine Kinder
myna kinnda
my Children

Countries and nationalities

Er ist Deutscher
*Air ist **doyt**sher*
He is a German

Sie ist Deutsche
Zee ist doytsha
She is a German

Woher kommen Sie?
*Vo**hair komm**en zee?*
Where do you come from?

Aus/Ich bin …
Owss/Ish bin …
From/I'm … (*in:* woman)

England ***eng**-lant* England	Engländer (in) ***eng**-lender (in)* English
Schottland ***shot**lant* Scotland	Schotte (Schottin) *shotta (shottin)* Scottish

Amerika/die U.S.A.
*a**mer**ika/dee oo.s.aa*
America/the U.S.A.

Amerikaner (in)
*ameri**kaa**ner (in)*
American

Australien
*ow**straa**lee-en*
Australia

Australier (in)
*ow**straa**lee-er (in)*
Australian

Kanada
***kan**ada*
Canada

Kanadier (in)
*ka**naa**dee-er (in)*
Canadian

Neuseeland
*noy**zay**lant*
New Zealand

Neuseelander (in)
*noy**zay**lander (in)*
New Zealander

Irland ***eer**lant* Ireland	Ire (Irin) *eera (**eer**in)* Irish
Wales *waylss* Wales	Waliser (in) *va**lee**ser (in)* Welsh

Around the clock and greetings

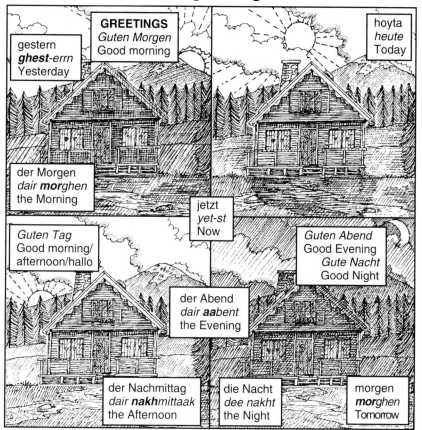

GREETINGS
Guten Morgen
Good morning

gestern
ghest-errn
Yesterday

hoyta
heute
Today

der Morgen
*dair **morghen***
the Morning

jetzt
yet-st
Now

Guten Tag
Good morning/
afternoon/hallo

Guten Abend
Good Evening
Gute Nacht
Good Night

der Abend
*dair **aab**ent*
the Evening

der Nachmittag
*dair **nakh**mittaak*
the Afternoon

die Nacht
dee nakht
the Night

morgen
morghen
Tomorrow

Days of the week — *dee vokha* — die Woche

Montag
***moan**taag*
Monday

Donnerstag
***donn**erstaag*
Thursday

Dienstag
***deens**taag*
Tuesday

Freitag
***fry**taag*
Friday

Mittwoch
***mit**vokh*
Wednesday

Samstag/
Sonnabend
***zams**taag/*
***zonn**aabent*
Saturday

Sonntag
***zonn**taag*
Sunday

Seasons, months and weather

im Frühling	im **fruw**ling	in spring

es ist windig
*ess ist **vind**ish*
it's windy

es regnet
*ess **rayg**-net*
it's raining

März
mairts
MARCH

Ostern
ohsterrn
Easter

April
*app**rill***
APRIL

Mai
my
MAY

im Sommer	im **zomm**er	in summer

die Sonne scheint
dee zonna shine-t
it's sunny

schönes Wetter
shurnas **vett**er
fine weather

Juni
yoonee
JUNE

Juli
yoolee
JULY

August
*ow-**goost***
AUGUST

im Herbst	im hairpst	in autumn/fall

die Ernte
dee airn-ta
the harvest

es ist kalt
ess ist kalt
it is cold

mir ist kalt
meer ist kalt
I'm cold

September
*sep**tem**ber*
SEPTEMBER

Oktober
*ok**tohb**er*
OCTOBER

November
*no**vem**ber*
NOVEMBER

im Winter	im **vin**ter	in winter

fröhliche
Weihnachten!
frurlisha
vynakhten!
Merry Christmas!

es schneit
ess shnyte
it's snowing

ein gutes
neues Jahr!
*ine **goo**tass
noyass yar!*
Happy New Year!

Dezember
*det**sem**ber*
DECEMBER

Januar
yannoo-ar
JANUARY

Februar
febroo-ar
FEBRUARY

Time

Wie spät ist es?
Vee shpayt ist ess?
What's the time?

Es ist drei Uhr
Ess ist dry oor
<u>It's three o'clock</u>

fünf (Minuten) nach drei
fuwnf (minooten) nakh dry
<u>five (minutes) past</u> three

zehn nach vier
tsayn nakh feer
<u>ten past</u> four

Viertel nach fünf
feertle nakh fuwnf
<u>quarter past</u> five

zwanzig nach sechs
tsvantsish nakh zex
<u>twenty past</u> six

fünf vor halb acht
fuwnf for halp akht
<u>twenty-five past</u> seven

halb neun
halp noyn
<u>half-past</u> eight

fünf nach halb neun
fuwnf nakh halp noyn
<u>twenty-five to</u> nine

zwanzig vor zehn
tsvantsish for tsayn
<u>twenty to</u> ten

Viertel vor elf
feertle for elf
<u>quarter to</u> eleven

tsayn for tsvurlf
zehn vor zwölf
<u>ten to</u> twelve

fuwnf for **eye**-nss
fünf vor eins
<u>five to</u> one

How German Works:
A Case of Agreement

Things: Nouns. In German all nouns are thought of as either masculine (m), feminine (f) or neuter (n). They always begin with a capital letter.

When talking about one thing only, i.e. a **singular** (s) item, **A** is ein (m), eine (f) or ein (n), e.g. — ein Junge (a boy), eine Straße (a street), ein Kind (a child). If there is more than one, i.e. in the **plural** (pl) most nouns change their endings, e.g. — Jungen (some boys), Straßen (some streets), Kinder (some children).
   (German doesn't usually bother with a word for "some").

The singular is der (m): der Junge (the boy)
               die (f): die Strasse (the street)
               das (n): das Kind (the child)

If the noun is plural, use die for all three genders, i.e.—
   die Jungen (the boys)
   die Straßen (the streets)
   die Kinder (the children)

Cases: English uses two words to say "of the", "to the", whereas German rolls them into one word, e.g. des Kindes: of the child, dem Kind: to the child. These short forms are called cases. Two of the four cases are used extensively in this book, the nominative (which is what you find if you look up a word in a dictionary) and the accusative or object case. The nominative is the person who does things, and the accusative is what they are done to, e.g.—
   Der Mann trinkt den Wein. The man (nominative) drinks the wine (accusative).

Describing things: Adjectives. If a noun is masculine the adjective describing it will be too. If a noun is feminine or neuter, or there are more than one, the ending will change slightly, to agree with the case of the noun, e.g.—
   ein kleiner Junge (a small boy)
   eine kleine Straße (a small street)
   ein kleines Kind (a small child)

This is dieser with masculine nouns, diese with feminine ones, dieses with neuters and diese in the plural.

It's mine: Possessive adjectives
The word for "my", "your", etc., depends on whether the **following** word is masculine, feminine, neuter or plural, e.g.—
   mein Hund (my dog), meine Hunde (my dogs).

	m and n	f and pl		m and n	f and pl
my	mein	meine	our	unser	unsere
(*your	dein	deine)	(your	euer	eure)
his	sein	seine	their	ihr	ihre
her	ihr	ihre	your (polite)	Ihr	Ihre

*see note on You under pronouns

People or things: Pronouns

"I", "you" (ich, Sie) etc. are shown with the verbs.
N.B. **You:** as a rule you should use Sie whether talking to one person or several, since du is used only with children, close friends and family (to you = Ihnen). **Me:** being part of the case system, me = mich, to me = mir.

Doing things: Verbs

Endings vary according to who is doing the action.

to be	sein	to come	kommen
I am	ich bin	I come	ich komme
(you are	du bist)	(you come	du kommst)
he/she/it is	er/sie/es ist	he/she/it comes	er/sie/es kommt
we are	wir sind	we come	wir kommen
(you are	ihr seid)	(you come	ihr kommt)
You/they are	Sie/sie sind	You/they come	Sie/sie kommen

to have	haben	to go	gehen
I have	ich habe	I go	ich gehe
(you have	du hast)	(you go	du gehst)
he/she/it has	er/sie/es hat	he/she/it goes	er/sie/es geht
we have	wir haben	we go	wir gehen
(you have	ihr habt)	(you go	ihr geht)
You/they have	Sie/sie haben	You/they go	Sie/sie gehen

to be able	können	to have to	müssen
I can	ich kann	I must	ich muß
(you can	du kannst)	(you must	du mußt)
he/she/it can	er/sie/es kann	he/she/it must	er/sie/es muß
we can	wir können	we must	wir müssen
(you can	ihr könnt)	(you must	ihr müßt)
You/they can	Sie/sie können	You/they must	Sie/sie müssen

Saying No: just add "nicht", e.g.—
"Ich kann nicht" (I can't).
"Es gefällt mir nicht" (I don't like it).

Asking Questions is very simple. Take the basic statement "Sie sprechen Englisch" (You speak English) and turn it round:
"Sprechen Sie Englisch?" (Do you speak English?)

Index

Dictionary

Live

Lost Property

Side Dishes

Sightseeing

Youth hostel

Numbers

0 null *nooll*	17 siebzehn *zeep-tsayn*	70 siebzig *zeep-tsish*
1 eins *eye-nss*	18 achtzehn *akht-tsayn*	80 achtzig *akht-tsish*
*2 zwei *tsv-eye*	19 neunzehn *noyn-tsayn*	90 neunzig *noyn-tsish*
3 drei *dry*	20 zwanzig *tsvantsish*	100 hundert *hoondert*
4 vier *feer*	21 einundzwanzig *ine oont tsvantsish*	101 hunderteins *hoondert eye-nss*
5 fünf *fuwnf*	22 zweiundzwanzig *tsv-eye oont tsvantsish*	200 zweihundert *tsv-eye hoondert*
6 sechs *zex*	23 dreiundzwanzig *dry oont tsvantsish*	1000 tausend *towzent*
7 sieben *zeeben*	24 vierundzwanzig *feer oont tsvantsish*	1001 tausendundeins *towzent oont eye-nss*
8 acht *akht*	25 fünfundzwanzig *fuwnf oont tsvantsish*	2000 zweitausend *tsv-eye towzent*
9 neun *noyn*	26 sechsundzwanzig *zex oont tsvantsish*	1000000 eine Million *eye-na mill-yone*
10 zehn *tsayn*	27 siebenundzwanzig *zeeben oont tsvantsish*	
11 elf *elf*	28 achtundzwanzig *akht oont tsvantsish*	
12 zwölf *tsvurlf*	29 neunundzwanzig *noyn oont tsvantsish*	
13 dreizehn *dry-tsayn*	30 dreißig *dry-sish*	
14 vierzehn *feer-tsayn*	40 vierzig *feer-tsish*	1st erste *airsta*
15 fünfzehn *fuwnf-tsayn*	50 fünfzig *fuwnf-tsish*	2nd zweite *tsv-eye-ta*
16 sechzehn *zekh-tsayn*	60 sechzig *zekh-tsish*	3rd dritte *dritta*

*see p.16